A HATTER GOES MAD!

Kristina Howells

Luton Town Footballers, Officials and
Supporters Talk to a Female Fan

First published November 1997 by
The Book Castle
12 Church Street
Dunstable, Bedfordshire, LU5 4RU

© Kristina Howells, 1997.

ISBN 1 871199 58 1
Designed by Trevor Wood, Houghton Regis, Beds.
Computer typeset by Keyword, Aldbury, Hertfordshire.
Printed and bound by Bookcraft (Bath) Ltd.

Front cover:
David Oldfield and Graham Alexander celebrate a goal against Crewe
Alexandra (AH).
Kristina Howells at Kenilworth Road, wearing the 1997/98 away strip
(GO).

Back cover:
Luton Town at home in 1907 (LN).

Contents

Foreword

Being associated with Luton Town F. C. was without doubt one of the highlights of my career.

As we know, the football club is an intimate part of the community, and to be part of that helped endear myself to the local people.

The warmth, care and loyalty that the directors, staff and everyone connected with the club, especially the supporters, showed to me, will live with me forever. And I am sure I speak for the majority of Luton Town F. C. players, past and present.

Mick Harford

Mick Harford

Here are some of the Junior Hatters at an away game in 1996. AH

Introduction

Well, a decade or two ago, who would have thought women would be getting so involved in the wonderful game of football?

In the 1990s you can see women watching it, playing it, reporting on it, running it, and now writing on the national sport that is predominantly a man's game. However, if we look back to the 1950s, the only female involvement in the game would be to watch it. Women were strictly taboo when it came to working in such a male domain. So why would women want to be interested in a man's sport? Well, for one thing, women are getting tired of men treating them as second best, and putting football first. So instead, if you can't beat them join them. Also, with improving facilities and a less intimidating atmosphere, the rest of the family is increasingly joining their man at a sport that they all love.

Being a Luton Town fan, even though for so few years, I have already endured many heartaches. So why be a Luton fan? Well I was born in Luton on July 14 1972, and have lived in the neighbouring town, Dunstable, most of my life. I can remember at the age of twelve getting a football sticker album with my brother, and seeing Luton Town in it. This only inspired me to collect them all, and also my local enthusiasm was a good way of shutting up the Arsenal and Tottenham fans at my middle school.

When I was away at university, I resisted the temptation to follow a more glamorous club and maintained my support for my local professional club. Unfortunately I couldn't afford to see Luton play live whilst a student. Yet my heart was always with the club, though I have only been able to become a regular supporter, following Luton Town both at home and away, since I finished university in 1995.

Why write a book on Luton? Well, I wanted to wallow in the club's recent history through meeting the people who work, play and support a team such as Luton. It is through their words that I can tell the tale of why thousands follow the Town.

This book takes us through some of our most memorable successes and defeats, as well as bringing the stories behind seeing them play up and down the country. I am grateful to all those who agreed to meet me and who passed on their most vivid memories and impressions of the club. And their enthusiasm on the one hand and their tribulations on the other could be echoed at football grounds the length and breadth of Britain. And increasingly it is a passion shared by both sexes!

Chapter 1

The Modern Luton Fan

Every Luton Town supporter has best and worst memories of following the Hatters. And the modern fan of Luton Town F. C. is going through the same feelings as did the '60s fan. This is because, in the 1960s, Luton suffered relegation from the top division to the bottom of the lowest and narrowly missed being kicked out of the football league altogether. Similarly, in the 1990s, in the space of four years, we have twice suffered painful relegation.

However, Luton Town F. C. are yet again proving to the nation that we are a good footballing team. And this led to obtaining a place in the 1997 play-offs for promotion straight back up into Division 1. Sadly, despite all the pomp and circumstance of the 1996/97 season, Luton Town F. C. was unable to get past the play-off semi-final. So we will just have to wait and see if we can accomplish it in the 1997/98 season!

Just why did Luton get relegated in the first place? Over the last few years we have had three chairmen and five managers. In 1990 David Evans left and Jim Smith took over as chairman. Then in 1991, David Kohler became the present chairman of Luton Town F. C. As for the managers, between 1990–1992, we had Ray Harford, Jimmy Ryan, and David Pleat, who stayed until the start of the 1995/96 season before going on to Sheffield Wednesday.

Then in 1995, David Kohler appointed an in-house manager, Terry Westley, whose only experience with a first team was when he coached the Ipswich side, not Luton. With Luton he had impressed in managing the youths rather successfully, but when given the job of first team manager he was not quite ready to meet the increased demands.

However this was soon rectified towards the end of 1995 with the appointment of a much more experienced manager, Lennie Lawrence. At the start of the new year he managed to get Luton temporarily away from relegation via an undefeated run of eight games. Yet despite Lennie's best efforts and intentions, it was not ultimately possible to avoid relegation in 1996.

Lennie Lawrence signs his autograph for the modern fan. AH

However, during the 1996/97 season, Lennie did a marvellous job in bringing Luton within grasp of instant promotion straight back up into Division 1, after what looked like a dodgy start to the season. Luton was only defeated in three league games between September 1996 and February 1997. And after fifteen years, we hit the number one spot in a division. Even if it was only for three days and then three hours over Christmas.

Let's now look at the differences between the two seasons by comparing two fanzine editions, which will show just how much Luton Town F. C. has changed, in both the opinions of supporters and in the way Luton play! In looking at fanzine issue no. 31 1995, of Mad as a Hatter, one supporter has this to say about Terry Westley and his assistant, Mick McGiven:

'Come on Kohler, we have given Terry Westley enough chances to prove himself as our manager now, and time and time again he has picked a team that plays, well let's face it, not to their full potential. So it must say something about the management if we keep losing all the time. It's time for a change Kohler, he's had enough chances.

'I should blame McGiven for this point. But both seem to be encouraging a Watford style: hoof the ball and chase it, (except we don't bother chasing the ball) instead of the passing football that we are renowned for, and it is getting to us fans.

'Westley also does not have a clue on what he is going on about! He says we are capable of being a top six side – everyone else knows we have not got a chance of that unless we are in Division 2. He also said that once our main players are back from injury, we will start showing our full potential. So tell us now Mr Westley, now that all our players are back from injury (except John Taylor), why are we still putting on dire performances? (Second half of the Oldham match at home 1/11/95) and why do half the players run around like headless chickens? (Scott Oakes), not wanting to kick the ball on the occasions we actually have it.'

So let's look now to the commentary from the same fanzine on the match referred to between Luton Town and Oldham which resulted in a 1–1 draw, it says:

'The debut of seventeen year old Stuart Douglas was the highlight of this game; 10 minutes later he proceeded to kick the ball at the goalkeeper, while making it look like a shot that even earned him applause. He scored with five minutes of the first half left, after Marvin Johnson had headed the ball down for Stuart to put in the top corner.

'Half time came and the town (Douglas) got a standing ovation, as it now looked like we're back on the right track. After a humiliating performance against Stoke, Charlton, etc., where we were absolutely awful. We came out in the second half and tried to sit on a one goal lead.

'What has Westley told them in his half time talk? "Right, lads, we are one goal up. So obviously we've got this game won. This will help push us up in the top six of the table. Don't bother going forward in this half, just defend.

"And you, Douglas, I was appalled by your performance, you were far too good for my team. You'd better have an average/less than average half or you will be straight off to be replaced by David Oldfield."

'So the Luton players took in this information and played like we have done in previous performances. Sixty-five minutes came and Ian Feuer made a world class save to deny Oldham. After thinking he had done enough to stop them scoring, the defence let him down again by standing and watching Halle put the ball straight into the net, past a stranded Feuer.

'Oldham then threatened to take all three points with numerous attacks that split our defence in two, (well one-and-a-half, as we only play a three man defence).

'Oldham should have scored, but their forwards seemed to be as good as Gavin Johnson up front. We came to life during injury time, when on a rare venture into the Oldham half, Ceri Hughes' 20-yard screamer was somehow saved by Gerrard, who tipped it over the bar. The referee was again, like at nearly all Luton games, a joke. What is the point of being so insistent on the stretcher rule, only when it is one of our players down? But as soon as an Oldham player gets injured, the referee allows him over five full minutes of on the field treatment, then lets him continue playing without even booking him. It can be said that nearly all referees at Luton matches need to learn the rules, before being allowed to officiate games.

'In concluding, the first half held out hope for us long-suffering Town fans. But overall we produced the same awful result we have been used to, week in week out.'

Away from the doom and gloom of the earlier fanzine, we now look to fanzine no. 39 of Mad as a Hatter that will shed better light on the 1996/97 season. A year after fanzine no. 31, one supporter says:

'Being a Saturday afternoon footballer myself, I don't get the chance to see the Town as often as I would like. However, I still consider myself a Luton Town fanatic, something I will remain until my dying day.

'Anyway the point I would like to make is, thanks Lennie for turning it around! You see, living in Sleaford near Lincoln, which appears to be a well-known bastion of Man. Utd. fans of whom half have no idea how to get to Manchester, but still wear the shirt; so you see I have taken my fair share of abuse.

'The majority of last season was spent receiving abuse as our results progressively got worse, i.e. "Ha, ha, you've lost again Dave!" was a favourite saying, as well as "Going down by the look of it" – another original. Well, I took all the jibes 'cause I figured the good times were not far away.

'So, here I am on 5th January 1997 with my team 2nd in the league and we're still in the F.A. Cup. But the best thing by far is the fact that those same United fans have, albeit grudgingly, had to accept that "they are going well this year Dave!" I now no longer dread 4.45pm and final score – in fact, I look forward to it, and it doesn't seem to matter too much if I lost the game I played in, as long as Luton won. I suppose what I really want to say is, thanks to the team and Lennie for putting a smile back on my face, and giving me a bit of "football pride".'

Luton Town players celebrating a winning goal. AH

In looking at a commentary from the same fanzine on the match between Luton Town and Notts County, that resulted in a 2–1 win, it says:

'An interesting trip this one. Some good beers, then the Notts scored first, and it looked like being the only goal. But they decided to try and hang on and Luton at last showed signs of waking up. Hughes scored with a rather speculative effort which seemed to go through the Notts keeper, and suddenly we believed we could win it.

'With two minutes remaining a pin-pointed pass by Oldfield found Alexander on the end of the pass, and he duly smacked it home to send the travelling 1,400 fans delirious . . . "Ohh ah Alexander, ooh ah Alexander" was the chant. A lucky win and it was good to see that Lennie laid into the lads after this performance – totally deserved.I think Notts County will have the best ground in the third division next year.'

In looking back at the 1995/96 season the major plus point that came out of Terry Westley as Luton's manager was the signing of our goalkeeper, Ian Feuer. Ian has made some tremendous saves, and because of this, he often gave Luton a chance of either drawing or winning a match.

The run of luck in the 1995/96 season was typical of fate working against us. If we look at our cup form, we lost out early on in the Coca-Cola Cup and Anglo Italian Cup, not forgetting our worst defeat, 7–1 to Grimsby in the F.A. Cup.

Then just as Luton seemed to be picking itself up on league form under our new manager Lennie Lawrence, enjoying one run of eight undefeated games, our leading striker of that season, Dwight Marshall, broke his leg in a game against Sunderland away on the 24 February 1996. And this meant he was out for the rest of that season and the start of the 1996/97 season.

When the 1996/97 season had just started the modern Luton fan thought that history was repeating itself, when we found ourselves yet again at the bottom of the table. But as the season went on, Luton fans became ever more hopeful that Luton could be in contention for the play-offs if not automatic promotion. Finally as the season drew to a close Luton Town was now in a play-off place with only one aim in mind, Division 1.

So how was this possible? It was possible due to the fact that we did not have to sell a player, and there was no change of manager. Luton Town players looked very confident on the pitch, with our best game of the season being at home to Crewe whereby we beat them 6—0. This result not only encouraged the players but it also encouraged the fans into believing that Luton were favourites for promotion back into Division 1, with one supporter saying:

'If you are one of the teams at the top of the league, luck is always with you compared to that of teams at the bottom of the table.' Which we all know is a very true statement!

The modern Town fans cheering on the team. AH

So anyway, let's now look further back into Luton's past, through some of the first-hand experiences people have had of Luton Town F. C. over recent decades. We begin with supporters who can remember games as far back as the thirties.

Chapter 2

The Town Before the '50s

There are relatively few people who can remember the Town before the '50s. However, there are some such supporters still alive today to tell of their tale in following the Town. Because of these experiences and a devotion to the club for all these years, despite Luton falling into bad times, they will never give up their love of the club. And this love forms the core from which tradition is passed onto future generations of supporters, as it similarly has been ever since Luton Town F. C. was first formed in 1885.

Cyril Pepper

I have supported Luton Town F. C. since 1931. I saw the game against Bristol Rovers in 1936, when Joe Payne scored ten goals against them, and I can remember when Luton had their first ever black player in the '30s; his name was George Parish.

However, it was after the war that I began to watch Luton more seriously, as I was in the Royal Navy until 1946. In 1946, when I got leave from the Navy I saw Luton play Derby County in a friendly; we lost that game. Then in 1947, Dally Duncan became Luton's manager, and eight years later, in 1955, Luton won a place in the first division for the first time ever in their history.

In 1955 we played at home to Sunderland, and had beaten them 8–1. This is one of many games that stand out for me, because Sunderland hadn't been beaten in so many weeks, and they were a very good team then, So it was really good to see

Here is Joseph Payne in a Luton shirt when he played for Luton Town F. C. in the '30s. LN

Luton get a result like this. Yet it has always been the team of 1955 that has stood out the most for me, and is one of my favourite Luton teams.

The 1961 game against Man. City will always stand out for me, especially when Dennis Law scored six past us. The game was abandoned halfway through due to heavy rain, the like I have not seen before. When we replayed that game a few weeks later, we were able to beat them. Yet it still didn't stop Mr Law getting another past us.

Well, since being a Luton fan, I have seen many great players go on to win international status whilst playing for Luton, but there is one thing for sure, life is never dull, being a Luton fan.

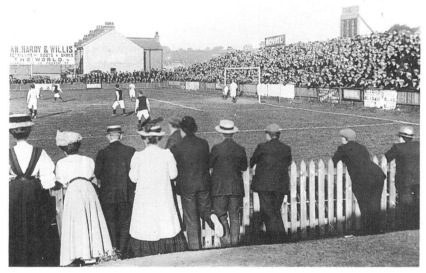

A Luton Town F. C. match at home in 1907. LN

Harry Whalley

I cannot remember when I first saw Luton play, it has been that long.

However I do remember a game we played in 1949 in particular. It was against Leicester City in the F.A. Cup; we drew at home 5–5. In the replay away at Leicester, they went on to win 5–3. Then they went on to win the cup after beating Wolves.

I can remember when Luton played Middlesborough in the '70s, we drew 3–3. It was a great game. Eric Morecambe was around then, he was a great man, and did much for the club, especially as he was able to build up the morale in the dressing room. We had a good run at the time of Alec Stock and Harry Haslem in the late '60s early '70s, and Eric Morecambe helped to make this run of results so special for Luton fans. Finally, I have seen many great games since I have been a Luton fan. But the worst game that I have seen is definitely against Millwall in 1985, and it is a game I never want to see happen, ever again.

Peter McCarthy

I have been a Luton fan since 1942, just before going into the Air Force. When I was in the Air Force I used to go with other local servicemen to watch Luton play. Yet it wasn't until after the war that I became a regular spectator.

Nowadays I am a little bit disillusioned with football in general because of the money aspect; it has been mentioned that smaller clubs such as Luton could become a nursery club for another team that has money.

However, proposals for a new stadium could take that scenario away and it should bring us more prosperity if it becomes reality. So with a new stadium, we could get into the Premiership, which will easily attract more people to support Luton as their team.

I have over the years seen so many games that bad ones are now just faded memories along with the good ones!

Bob Crawley

At present I am a steward at Luton Town F. C. I have been since 1986. I have also been a fan of Luton since the days of Billy Cooke in the 1940s. I was playing football myself at the time in the South Midlands league, yet I always used to try to watch a Luton game whenever I could.

My best moment in following the Town was when we won

the Littlewoods Cup against Arsenal in 1988. The atmosphere was brilliant both in the community and at the club. I went to Wembley to see them play twice: once in the final of the Simod Cup against Reading when we lost 4–1, and again in the Littlewoods Cup, when we beat Arsenal 3–2.

I am enjoying working for Luton Town, I find the supporters and everyone connected with the club to be great fun, and I am glad to be associated with Luton Town F. C.

1939/40. (Only playing personnel are named.)
Back row: *Gardner, Goodyear, Dunsmore, Wale, King, Fletcher, Mayberry, Coen, Strathie, Lutterloch, Ladd.*
Second Row: *Smith, Carr, Dreyer, Roberts, Hindmarsh, Duke, Campbell, Loughran, Finlayson, Nelson, Redfern.*
Third row: *Stephenson, Vinall, Carroll, Connelly, Billington, Gager.*
Front row: *Burgess, Duggan, Laing, Ferguson, Fullarton, Hogg, Clark. LN*
It is said that this team could have developed into Luton's best ever team. When war broke out in September 1939 Luton were top of Division 2, this after narrowly missing promotion at the end of the 1938/39 season. Of this team Coen, Ladd and Clark lost their lives during the war, whilst Carroll survived some six weeks on a makeshift raft after the ship on which he was serving was sunk. Of this team only Gardner, Goodyear, Duke, Connelly, Gager and Duggan resumed their careers at Luton after the war. Loughran played for Burnley after the war.

Chapter 3

1950s Onwards Relived

It was from the 1950s onwards that supporters began to remember clearly the matches that follow, and it was in this decade that Luton began to make its name as a footballing side in this country. The dedicated supporters that now follow go on to tell the tale of life during and after the 1950s.

Brian Swain

I am a local boy who has followed Luton all my life. I joined St. Johns as a kid in order to get in free at Kenilworth Road. Now I am sports editor for the Luton News, and report regularly on Luton Town's matches. This is a job that I've always wanted.

When I left school, I joined the Luton News, but I left after three years in 1958 for national service. Then a while later, I joined a paper in Manchester. I returned to Luton in 1962, and became sports editor after Eric Pugh died in 1972.

I still could not believe my luck in being paid to watch Luton Town, having previously spent thousands doing so! I had helped Eric on match days before he died, and since taking on the job I have not missed a single league, or F.A. Cup match, a total of well over one thousand consecutive games. (I only missed one Anglo Italian Cup game because no one would take up my offer of sharing the petrol to drive to Cesena in November 1995.)

The strangest day out was on January 13 1987. It was snowing like hell, and Luton were due to play at Anfield in an F.A Cup replay. The police advice was not to drive in a blizzard, so the club hired a plane to fly from Heathrow. Because of weather delays everyone had to sit waiting for hours, and it still failed to get away in time. I left Luton instead by road at 10am, ignoring the police advice, and struggled up north to arrive at Anfield at 5pm, just as the local radio announced that the game was called off because the team and John Moore were snowed in. Kenny Daglish went potty, and was more than keen to give me an interview: 'If you could get here, so can they', he said, 'Yes', I replied, 'but would you want your team to play a big Cup tie after seven hours on the road?' 'But we've bought the meat pies, we'll have to give them away . . .' 'Tough luck'. I got home to Luton at 4am the next day. The Town had drawn 0–0 at Kenilworth Road, and the delayed replay was eventually another 0–0 at Anfield on January 28. Finally the tie's result was LUTON 3 (Stein, Harford pen, Newell) LIVERPOOL 0. Daglish was livid, and gave a famous moaning TV interview, 'They should not be in it' was his complaint. Which gave rise to a famous joke: 'What is the difference between a Boeing 707 and Kenny Daglish? The Boeing stops whining when it gets to Luton . . .' The best game that I have seen was when Luton were away to Man. City, on May 14 1983, and Raddy Antic's winner came four minutes from the end of the season. Second best is the Littlewoods Cup win of 1988. However, I chose the Maine Road game in 1983 because that result was so important. It kept the Town in what is now the Premiership, at the start of a decade where they brilliantly lived above their means.

Nick Owen

I am an avid supporter of Luton Town F. C. I was born and bred in the town of Berkhamsted. The first match I saw was in 1958 with my father. I was only ten years old, and Luton was playing Leeds United at home. LUTON 1 LEEDS 1.

Allan Brown scored the goal for Luton. I found it to be a brilliant experience, and I wanted to see more. My best memories are of winning the Littlewoods Cup in 1988. It was a wonderful and an emotional day. But it was also a brilliant game. LUTON 3 ARSENAL 2.

It was the first time that I was able to take my parents to a game as my guest, all of thirty years since I first saw Luton.

Another favourite memory was when Luton won the 4th division in 1968, and became champions of the league with Bruce Rioch scoring the goals along with Malcolm MacDonald in the fight back to the top division.

My favourite game was when we were able to relegate Sheffield Wednesday by beating them 5-1 at Hillsborough with Malcolm MacDonald scoring a hat trick and Don Givens scoring the other two goals.

When I was away at university, I used to hitch-hike to see Luton play. I have hitch-hiked to Hartlepool and seen them lose by 1-0, also to Stockport. On that occasion I arrived very early to watch the match, and met up with a family man who took me to the game and fed me!

Since 1968, I have seen Luton play right up and down the country, and I've seen them lose so often. My worst memories are all about relegations, plus the semi-final against Everton in the F.A. Cup of 1985, where Everton were able to equalise and then won on penalties. It was rather a shattering experience because Luton played so well against them. Hill, Stein and Parker played at their best, and they looked wonderful.

In another game Luton played against Lincoln City away when we were at the foot of the old 4th Division. We lost that game by 8-1. My only disappointment at present concerns the ground, as a new stadium is what we need. But hopefully this will happen eventually. I found the building of the executive boxes to be rather odd. But I would like us to stay where we are and to expand on it in a big way.

I have had wonderful moments since supporting Luton, and if there was a change to the present stadium, in the sense that people thought it was a good ground, then we would get more support. Especially if there were much better facilities for parking and generally.

I have managed to convert my family into supporting Luton Town, which includes my two sons. And they all come as often as they can.

Shirley Hobbs

I have followed the Hatters pretty much all of my life. I was born in Luton and have stayed here ever since. All of my family have supported Luton Town, making me the third generation in being a Hatter.

In the latter part of the '40s, I can remember how supporters used to dress to attend a game. They did not wear their colours in those days, they wore very smart clothes accompanied by a rosette or a club scarf.

At the age of eleven, I started a new school, which was then known as Luton High School. I used to travel to school by bus, with another girl called Pat. Pat was an avid Luton fan, and every Monday all she could talk about was the match of the previous Saturday. Finally, at the age of thirteen, I decided to go with Pat to see my first game at Kenilworth Road on the 8 September 1951. My father took me into the ground via the entrance at the top of Kenilworth Road, before the new stand was built. I then met up with Pat to watch the game. Pat and I watched the game from the enclosure, sitting on the barrier wall.

In that season Luton was in Division 2. We were playing Notts. County on that day, and it resulted in a Luton win of 6–0. The players wore white shirts and black shorts. Due to this great result I thought, 'I like this, I want to see more'.

So the following week Luton were playing away to Q.P.R. My father drove me to the game. I can remember sitting quite high up in the old Loftus Road stadium in West London. The result of the game was: Q.P.R 0 LUTON 0.

After that, I used to regularly see Luton play at home, with Pat right up until we left school, but soon after that we lost contact.

However, I was able to take more friends to see Luton play. We soon moved from the enclosure to behind the goal, at the Kenilworth Road end.

We were quite close to the goalkeeper, Bernard Streten, who, whilst at Luton, was capped for England. He was a real character, and he made the most spectacular saves. The children and teenagers standing behind the goal with us used to throw sweets into it. Bernard kept the sweets given to him in an old tweed cap. But before picking up the sweets, he used to wave at the children. This happened at every home game whilst Bernard was in goal. The goalkeepers used to wear a green shirt, and shorts of the team's colours, with a straw cap.

Luton supporters parading near the Town Hall after the F. A. Cup final at Wembley in 1959. LN

By the end of the 1954/55 season, Luton Town were promoted into Division 1 for the first time ever in the club's history. We had to beat Doncaster away in order to win instant promotion on the last game of the season. And this we did comfortably. LUTON 3 DONCASTER 0.

Luton managed to hold their own in Division 1 for two to three seasons. In the 1958/59 season, Luton Town reached the Cup final. And this was the season when I was able to see every home and away game.

To get to the Cup final, Luton first played Leeds in the third round, and we won at home. The 4th round was against Leicester, where we drew at home and won away. After that, Luton had Ipswich in the fifth round and won again.

Then in the sixth round, Luton drew Blackpool away. British Rail was able to lay on a special train service for the Luton fans, and I went to the game with a friend called Margaret. After half-time Luton were winning 1–0, but in the second half, when Ken Hawkes went to pass the ball to Ron Baynham, a Blackpool player intervened and scored the equaliser.

There was no penalty shoot out in those days. So the replay was to take place at Kenilworth Road a week later. The game was held on a Wednesday afternoon. This was to be Luton's first real chance of a semi-final in a Cup competition, so the town did their best to support Luton in the replay. During the game Allan Brown scored the only goal for Luton. The crowd went mad after the final whistle. Luton now had to play Norwich in the semi-finals. Norwich at the time was only the second third division team ever to make it into the semi-finals of the Cup competition (with York as the first before them). The whole country was behind this game, hoping that Norwich would make it to the Cup final. The game was played at White Hart Lane. During the game, Norwich played with a lot of confidence, and because of this the game resulted in a 1–1 draw. The replay was to take place at St. Andrews, Birmingham on 18 March 1959. During the game Bingham scored the only goal for Luton, making the result: LUTON 1 NORWICH 0.

Now that Luton had made it to the Cup final against Nottingham Forest, the shops and the Town Hall in Luton were decorated in the team's colours, black and white. Before the

1959 F. A. Cup final against Nottingham Forest. LN

final, Luton had beaten Nottingham Forest 5–1 in the league. So naturally people thought we could beat them again. But sadly we lost 2–1.

Between the years 1951–1956, I can remember when the Town beat both Wolves 5–1 and Sunderland 8–1 at home. When we played Wolves on a cold November day in 1955, some of the children who attended that game were lifted out of the terraces and put onto the gravel path, alongside the pitch. This was done so that more Luton supporters could see the game.

During the time I have followed the Town, I have seen them play all over the country. I am so glad that my father first showed me his interest in following Luton Town.

My favourite games are all Cup games and winning promotion. With my worst games naturally being relegation and defeat.

Bob Morton

I signed for Luton Town F. C. as a part-time professional at the age of eighteen, in February 1946, and stayed for twenty years. When I first signed for Luton, there were around 40–50 other semi-professional footballers, who had been re-employed after serving in the armed forces during the War. If the club had not re-employed some of these men, then they would be breaking the law and a hefty fine could be placed on them.

My highlights at Luton have been firstly winning promotion into the first division, plus playing for the England B team against Northern Ireland and Russia, as well as scoring some of the goals in a first division match in the 1955/56 season against Sunderland, where we had won 8–1.

My biggest disappointment whilst playing for Luton was losing to Nottingham Forest in the 1959 F.A. Cup final. We had a good record against Nottingham Forest, and on the day Luton just didn't have enough steam to beat them.

When I played for Luton there were no substitutions allowed as in today's game, so if a player got injured and I was playing in a number 12 shirt, I would not have got a game.

My dislikes are losing to clubs that we should have beaten. But I enjoyed playing professional football, and I'm pleased that it was with Luton Town F. C.

The official photograph that appeared in the Luton News dated Tuesday 3rd May 1955, showing the players and officials of the club who were involved in the promotion season 1954/55. LN

Team 1955 Division 1 promotion

Back row: G Cummins, A Collier, R Morton, B Streten, C Watkins, R Baynham, W Shanks, W Dallas.

2nd row: T Mackey (Ast. Trainer), A Taylor, N Arnison, R Davies, P Macevan, J Scott, T Kelly, A Thomson, H Wright (Trainer), T Kelly (snr.) (Ast. Team Trainer).

3rd row: Mr P Coley (Secretary), M Cullen, R Smith, J Adams, G Turner, D Allen, S Dunne, J Pemberton, J Groves, D Duncan (Manager).

Front row: Mr T Hodgson, Mr P Wright, B A Herne, Mr A England, J Pye, Mr P Mitchell (Chairman), S Owen (Captain), Mr H Richardson, B Mitchell, Mr H Hewson, Dr E Crarer.

Wally Shanks

I came to Luton Town F. C. in 1946 from Chelsea, and I left in 1960. It was Joe Payne who first introduced me to the club following a meeting with him. He said: 'The manager of Luton Town F. C., George Martin, is interested in you as a player, and wants to sign you.'

At first I didn't know what he was on about: where was this place Luton and why did he want to sign me? But I knew that my chances at Chelsea were rather limited, as they had over fifty players on their books, and were running three teams simultaneously. After Joe mentioned that the manager of Luton was interested in me, I asked him 'where Luton was'; he replied, 'Oh Wally, it's just outside London'. So I went up to Luton to see George Martin, and that's how it all started. But at the time, there was another club also interested in me. Luton Town knew this and offered by £2 a week more, so because of this I decided to play for Luton Town F. C.

I had some excellent times at Luton. My main highlight was being a part of the team that won the club promotion into the first division for the first time in its history, at the end of the 1954/55 season. It was a great year and I will always have fond memories of the games leading up to us winning promotion.

I found Luton a friendly club to be at, everyone got on well with each other, and there was a real sense of comradeship amongst the staff. I still keep in touch with some of the players from the '50s squad, but sadly many of them have passed away. We blended in well as a team and this can be seen as one of the major plus points that led to us being so successful at the time.

I have encountered many funny moments whilst playing for Luton over the fourteen years I was there. One such moment occurred whilst we were training. One of the players decided to put marzipan inside one of the player's pants without him knowing. Marzipan was used to soothe very painful injuries and was very hot. After training we all arranged to meet up in the local cafe nearby for a cup of tea, and wait for that particular player's reaction to the marzipan. He would have liked to sit down but came in and said, 'I can't, as my bottom is burning,' and went home. We just couldn't stop laughing; these were the kind of tricks we would play on one another that would heighten the team spirit.

Every football team in the country has its characters, and Luton was no exception. Bernard Streten was Luton's character at the time; he played in goal. Before coming to Luton, he was a P. E. instructor for the R.A.F. On match days Bernard would come racing out of the players' tunnel and somersault towards the goal. He would then stop for the crowd to cheer, before doing the final one into the goal. Off the pitch, Bernard was the biggest glutton you would ever meet. He was slim and fit, but he also ate enough food for an entire army. He was a real character, yet a very fine goalkeeper.

Ken Hawkes

I signed for Luton Town F. C. in the late 1950s and left in 1961. During this time I was called up for National Service into the Army.

My debut was in 1957 against West Bromwich Albion. An old friend of mine from schoolboy days, Bobby Robson the ex-England manager, was captain of the West Bromwich side in this game. We beat them 4–1.

My worst Luton match was against Sheffield Wednesday away. I played left back at the time, and I could handle most of the wingers in the first division. But in this particular match, a winger called Tom Finney gave me a right chasing! I could do nothing with him. Then in the return game at Kenilworth Road, he hardly got a touch of the ball.

During my spell at Kenilworth Road, the players didn't change as much as they do today. There were a recognised 14–15 players who got a regular place in the first team. There were no substitutions made either, so if you got injured you either left the field or struggled on the field.

There were a lot of laughs to be had at Luton Town F. C. My funniest moment concerned Wally Shanks. Now Wally was a real joker and a terrific guy. But he was always the one for messing about with the players' underpants. One day, Bob Morton was so fed up with Wally's antics that he took hold of his underpants and threw them over the fence on to the railway line. However, instead of the pants landing on the line, they ended up in a railway carriage. We just laughed so much, though Wally eventually got them back.

My main like about Luton was the fact that I was well received by the people of the town. Luton is a very homely club to be at. I disliked not being able to play in the first team all the time, and resented being transferred to Peterborough F. C. which I didn't like at all, Peterborough being completely different from Luton. It wasn't as homely and it seemed more like a factory job, where you just turned up, did what you had to, then went again.

The games leading up to the 1959 F. A. Cup final consisted mainly of draws, which we won at the second replay. My most horrific moment in the competition was in the sixth round against Blackpool away. Stanley Mathews was playing for them then, and I had to try and stop him from getting hold of the ball. With about ten seconds left before the final whistle, Luton was 1–0 in front and we decided to keep hold of the ball. I had the ball at the time, when I heard Ron Baynham call to me 'let's have it'; just as I was about to play the ball to him, Dave Pacey said 'don't do it'. This put me off, and I ended up not playing the ball at all. Then just as their left-footed centre forward was about to take the ball off me, he slipped. Whilst he was lying on the ground his toe barely touched the ball, which trickled past Ron Baynham, hit the post and went into the goal. At the final whistle the game ended 1–1. I could have died; I had been under no pressure to play the ball and yet I allowed myself to be put off by another player.

The replay was played the following Wednesday at Kenilworth Road. Blackpool complained about Luton's floodlights and got the game moved to a 2.00pm kick-off. The attendance was over 30,000. The ground was absolutely packed; how all these supporters got in I will never know. During the match a former Blackpool player, Allan Brown, scored the only goal of the game against his old club, which was enough to take Luton through to the semi-finals. Eventually we reached the final. The same eleven players who played in the final had played in all the earlier rounds of the F.A. Cup competition.

On the day of the final, Luton had made a big mistake. We didn't prepare at all well for the match, and this was due to the fact that Luton didn't have a real manager at the time. Frank King the physio, a couple of directors, and Syd Owen the team captain were taking on the collective responsibility of managing

Luton. Before the Cup Final, the management went to various clubs who regularly played in Cup Finals at Wembley, and asked them for their advice on how Luton should go about preparing for the game. The advice that came back was for all the players to relax and the football will come. Which seemed obscure, as when I was a small boy playing in Cup Finals I could never relax. So consequently one of two of the players took this advice on board. During the Final against Nottingham Forest, they scored two early goals, but with the no substitution rule Forest went down to eight men through injury. Yet we still couldn't beat them. It wasn't our day in the end, but our inability to prepare for the game mean we hadn't deserved any better. This can be seen as my major disappointment; we had the opportunity to win the F.A. Cup but let ourselves down.

I have found the supporters of Luton Town F. C. to be terrific. They would follow you wherever you played in the country, by taking the special train. I found that there was as much support in the area outside Luton as there was in Luton.

The team was very close, and during the matches everyone backed one another up. If a player was struggling on the field, the rest of the team would help him out by doing something about it.

After training, we all used to go and play golf. It was great though we had more arguments over golf than we ever had about anything else. My younger brother Barry also played for Luton Town F. C. He wasn't able to play many games for the first team, but he stayed at Luton for about five seasons. He also enjoyed his time at Luton and found them to be the best years of his life.

It was very sad to hear the news that Gordon Turner amongst other Luton players in the team around the same time as me, had passed away. They were a great bunch of guys, and they will be greatly missed by all who knew and played with them. We had some fun times, and when I watch Luton play today, I will always remember the good times that I had whilst wearing a Luton shirt.

Chapter 4

Luton Hit Rock Bottom, 1960s

It was in the 1960s that Luton began to fade into the shadows. They were relegated from Division 1 in 1960. Then from Division 2 in 1963, as well as from Division 3 in 1965. But after a few years of struggling in Division 4, Luton won promotion back into Division 3 in 1968.

How did it come to go so wrong? Well, in the following season, 1959/60, Sid Owen became Luton Town's manager. He had a difficult job ahead of him, because the players in the first team were at or past their peak period. So after struggling in Division 1, Luton were relegated, and relegated until they could go no further. Yet despite this, Luton Town F. C. were still able to attract dedicated supporters and players, and a few now recall this difficult period.

Roger Wash

At present I am the club historian and statistician. I am a very keen supporter of Luton Town F. C., which is a big plus with respect to my involvement with the club.

So why be a Luton Town supporter? Being born in Ivy Road, Luton, and having a father and grandfather who followed the town certainly helped, as well as a great grandfather who died of pneumonia after standing out in the rain on the Kenilworth Road terrace in 1936! Such is the Wash family devotion to duty that my son, who was born in Watford, (fancy having that in your passport), is now a regular and a fifth-generation supporter.

My earliest memory of anything connected with the club was watching cranes lifting pieces of concrete terracing over the top of the Bobbers stand, when the Oak Road end was extended in 1956. This would make me four at the time!

From then on until 1960, vague snatches of matches are recalled with the opposition always wearing red and always scoring against us. The queues to get in would stretch way down Ivy Road, and my mother was always disgusted when men relieved themselves against the side of alleyways!

We often used to play cowboys and indians amongst the cars and the coaches, (a fertile imagination), that were parked on both sides of the road, before slipping into the ground shortly after half-time.

I can recall the F.A. Cup game against Northampton in 1961, and being lifted over the heads of people down to the front, (yes, it really did happen in those days); the cup game against Man. City when Dennis Law scored six with the match being abandoned after rain, the like of which I had not seen before. And the penalty save by Jim Standen against Ian St. John of Liverpool, when the ball hit his heel and ballooned over the bar.

By this time, I (along with other kids from my street) was a past master at sneaking into the ground without paying, either at the top of Kenilworth Road where the gateman was usually too engrossed in the game to spot us, or under the rusty corrugated iron fence that ran along the railway line.

We used to play football in the car park at the top of Kenilworth Road on non-match days, when the occupier of the top house used to threaten to put a knife through our ball. The occupier? None other than Joe Payne, of ten goal fame!

Most of our time used to be spent in or around Kenilworth Road, and on wet days we played football under the Kenilworth Road terrace until eventually chased off by groundsman Tom King, who was another happy, smiling ex-Town player.

By this time, though, we were taking a lot more interest in watching the games, and a group of us from Luton Grammar School were the original Oak Road choir; if you call it a choir, where you had a dozen people standing right at the front singing songs, in high-pitched voices, brazenly stolen from other clubs.

Over the succeeding thirty-odd years, I have many fond memories and some not so fond when watching the Town, although I haven't lived in Luton since 1974, having moved to Watford, Colchester, and for the last twelve years Newmarket. I have missed only a handful of home games, and see my share of games involving the team on its travels.

In no particular order, some of my highlights have been:

1. The 1967/68 season in general and particularly the early campaign win at Charlton in the League Cup, the first away win at Chester, the victory at Brentford that put us to the top of the league for the first time. The 1–0 triumph at Halifax that secured promotion, and the 4–0 thumping of Crewe at Kenilworth Road the following week which clinched the championship. It must be remembered that to the supporters of my generation, the fourth division title was the first success we had encountered, being a shade too young to fully appreciate the F.A. Cup run.

2. The early home games the following season, when we played some scintillating stuff and knocked in a hatful of goals.

3. The 1–0 win at Reading on the way to promotion from Division 3 in 1970. A tremendous end to end game, with the winner coming in the final moments from Malcolm MacDonald.

4. The early season 1–1 draw at Birmingham in 1970/71, in front of a 30,000 plus crowd. With this game we really knew we were back in the big time and could cope.

5. From the same season the 5–1 win at Sheffield Wednesday with Malcolm MacDonald scoring three and the 1–0 victory at Q.P.R. with Mike Keen scoring against his old club in the first minute.

6. The 2–0 win at Newcastle in the Cup in 1973. A tremendous effort.

7. The 1–1 draw at West Bromwich in 1974 that secured promotion back to Division 1, followed by the party night against Sunderland when the game could have ended ten all.

8. The home games during the second half of the 1974/75 season, when some of the biggest clubs in the country were steam-rollered into defeat.

9. A home game against Hull in 1976/77, when the Tigers held on to an early 1–0 lead until two goals in the dying seconds.

Hull assistant manager Andy Davidson was not best pleased, and offered to take on the crowd enclosure.

10. Ricky Hill's debut against Bristol Rovers in 1976, when he set up a goal and then scored with his first two touches of the ball.

11. A 3-3 draw with Chelsea on New Year's Day in 1980. Another game that could have broken the scoring records.

12. The promotion clinching game against Shrewsbury in 1982, and the 3-1 win over Norwich in the same season, when the Town went up in the first five minutes.

13. Paul Walsh's hat trick against Notts. County in 1982/83.

14. That win over Man. City!

15. Some of the home games during 1985/86, when Mick Harford and Brian Stein were at their peak. The Cup win over Arsenal and the league win over Manchester United stand out.

16. April 24 1988.

17. The 3-2 win at Derby in 1990. Another Houdini escape from relegation.

18. The Cup wins over Newcastle and West Ham in 1994.

Of course there have been more than a few disappointments along the way:

1. Just the whole period 1962-65, culminating in a 0-0 home draw with Workington, in front of just over 2,000 spectators, as we dropped into Division four.

2. The 1-1 draw at Chester in 1966 with a win guaranteeing promotion at the first attempt. Particularly galling as we had been 2-0 up at Sealand Road a few weeks earlier, when the match was abandoned.

3. An 8-1 defeat at Lincoln in 1966/67. We were one place off the bottom of Division 4, while they were below us!

4. Easter 1971 when we lost all three games and kissed promotion goodbye.

5. Tottenham beating Leeds 4-2 at White Hart Lane in 1975, thus sending us down from Division 1. I still find that scoreline hard to believe.

6. A dismal 3-0 defeat on a wet night at Leicester in 1979. I sincerely thought we were about to be relegated that season.

7. A 5-1 home defeat by Everton in 1982/83, with all the other strugglers winning, leaving us with mountains to climb.

8. The F.A. Cup semi-final defeat by Everton in 1985. I don't

think I have been so devastated before or since after losing, although it turned out to be a blessing in disguise as we channelled our efforts into avoiding relegation.

9. The Simod Cup final disaster in 1988.

10. Relegation at the end of the 1995/96 season.

Rather more highs than lows over the years, although you do tend to remember the good times. One thing is for certain, there will never be a dull moment in being a Luton Town supporter.

An aerial view of the Luton ground from the 60s. GO

John Moore

I am now Luton Town F. C. youth team manager. In 1965 I was on a free transfer from Motherwell F.C. I served three years there as a semi-pro until transferring to Luton Town F. C.

By the time David Pleat left Luton to go to Tottenham, I was already reserve team coach. And what with Mr Evans making a big thing about loyalties, I got the job as Luton's manager. My heart has always been with Luton Town since I joined. The club needed to continue the force it had built up at the time, and I had to hold the force together.

I didn't like being manager. I found that in my one year of being manager, I was in the office a lot and spent too much time getting involved with office work, instead of spending enough time with the players. We were successful in the first division when I was manager as we finished seventh in the league.

I did not like the job, and I left Luton for three years in 1987. In the 1989/90 season I joined Leicester City. Then in 1990 I returned to Luton Town as reserve team coach.

My greatest moment as a player was when Luton won the Division 4 championship in the 1968/69 season. And when Luton beat Newcastle in the F.A. Cup by 2–0 away, with Malcolm MacDonald playing against us.

As manager we were able to beat Liverpool by 4–1, then by 3–0, in the season of 1986. And finishing seventh in the league, (now the Premier), in that same season.

The worst moment was not being on the staff when Luton won the Littlewoods Cup for the first time in their history. And when Luton got relegated twice, once in 1992 after David Pleat's first season back. Then in 1996.

In 1974 Luton Town won promotion to the first division, and I was given a free transfer as a player. Then I came back in 1978. I like Luton Town F.C. It is a very small and friendly club where we work quite hard to produce our own young players by giving them the opportunity to play football with the senior staff.

My only dislike is the ground. Since 1965 Luton has been talking about relocation, etc., and they have never achieved it. If we had a new home we could probably make more of ourselves as a club.

Chapter 5

We're Aiming High, 1970s

Having spent the majority of the 1960s facing relegation and massive disappointments, Luton's fight to the top starts after they won promotion from Division 4 in 1968. It then took a further six years before Luton was once again playing in Division 1. A gap of some fourteen years from when they were last there.

Despite having only one season in Division 1, it was a great achievement. So here are some more supporters of the late '60s onwards.

Andrew Wallace

I was born in 1952 in Ickleford near Hitchin. My first visit to Kenilworth Road was in 1961, when I saw Luton draw 1–1 against Derby County. But I only became a regular supporter in 1968.

Since 1978, I have not missed a home match at Kenilworth Road, and I have travelled to around 40% of away matches. I have visited 106 league grounds, and was an early member of the 92 club. I have also seen Luton at 77 grounds, in addition to which I have visited 40 German grounds.

However my six best matches are as follows:
1. v SOUTHPORT (H) DIV 3 1970 1–0.
Having narrowly missed promotion to Division 2 the previous season, the Town had been six points clear at the top by Christmas. Yet had soon slipped back to just one point in front of Bristol Rovers. We had two more games to play, but in that

previous season, Southport had frustrated us with a 0–0 draw. It seemed as if history was going to repeat itself, as Luton were at a similar level in the table to the previous season. But after half an hour, Viv Busby scored a stunning goal at the Kenilworth Road end to break the deadlock.

The final score was 1–0 and on leaving the ground, we heard that Bristol Rovers had lost 2–1 at home to Gillingham. Then we only needed one point for promotion, and this was achieved with a goalless draw at Mansfield.

2. v NOTTINGHAM FOREST (H) F.A. CUP 3RD ROUND REPLAY 1971 3–4.

Having drawn 1–1 at first division Forest the previous Saturday, all thanks to a Malcolm MacDonald equaliser. This game was an absolute thriller. Forest took the lead only for MacDonald to equalise. They then took a 3–1 lead, but two further MacDonald goals bought it back to 3–3. Yet only a few minutes from the end, Forest scored the winner.

The crowd of 23,483 created a brilliant atmosphere and were preparing for extra time almost immediately, when Duncan

A game in the '70s. GO

McKenzie shot the winner right at the end. It can be seen as the most exciting game that I have ever seen, even if it did end in defeat.

3. v BIRMINGHAM CITY (H) DIV 2 1971 3–2.

Both clubs were in the thick of the promotion race. There was a crowd of around 25,172 including 7,000 from Birmingham, who paraded their new discovery – a certain Trevor Francis. Birmingham quickly took the lead by two goals, but the Town were level by half-time with Viv Busby as Luton's scorer. The winner early in the second half was from a free kick by Allan Clough. Which now meant that the Town's promotion dream was very much still alive. Until Easter, when they just narrowly missed promotion.

4. v MANCHESTER CITY (A) DIV 1 1983 1–0.

This game will be so well known to all Town fans, and many other fans who were there to witness it. I had adopted a pessimistic stance after the Everton and Manchester United defeats, which had occurred during the previous week. So I would not have been all that disappointed if Luton had gone down.

When Raddy Antic scored the famous goal, I immediately thought there must be around seven minutes left. But on a closer inspection of the watch, there were only four minutes left, and my reaction was, 'Surely we can hold on'. Which of course we safely did.

5. v ARSENAL, LITTLEWOODS CUP FINAL AT WEMBLEY IN 1988 3–2.

Undoubtedly the Town's greatest moment in their history. Following on the time theme from Main Road in 1982 – when Brian Stein scored the winner. I thought there were still nine minutes left. Then suddenly the referee blew the whistle for full time, and all the dreams of fellow supporters had come true.

6. v DERBY COUNTY (A) DIV 1 1990 3–2.

After Maine Road in 1982, our second great escape. I felt that we could somehow win. When Luton took a 2–0 lead and Sheffield Wednesday seemed to be losing to Nottingham Forest, it looked to be our day but we then had to suffer a Derby comeback to 2–2, before Kingsley Black scored the winner with fifteen minutes to go.

The players gave their absolute all, and who can forget Mick

Kennedy's corner flag tricks as time ran out. The 5,000 Luton fans made it a wonderful day to remember.

My six worst matches are as follows:

1–3. EASTER 1970 DIVISION 2.

BRISTOL CITY (A) 2–3.

MILLWALL (A) 0–4.

LEICESTER CITY (H) 1–3.

When Good Friday 1970 came, the Town had a strong possibility of winning promotion for the second year running, and when we led 2–0 at Ashton gate at half-time, albeit slightly fortunately, one could start dreaming of Division 1. Sadly three Bristol goals in five minutes turned the game around. We had plenty of time after the game to reflect on it whilst standing in the rain at Ashton Gate Halt, waiting for the football special train back to Luton. The next day, Easter Saturday, saw the worst performance of the season, when the Town was thrashed 4–0 by an ordinary Millwall side. Still, all was not lost when one of our promotion rivals, Leicester City, came to Kenilworth Road. The crowd of 24,405 saw Luton take the lead in the first minute with an own goal past Peter Shilton in the Oak Road end. However, chances were missed and eventually Leicester City went on to win 3–1. They made promotion, but the Town now knew that they had missed out after three Easter defeats.

4. v SUNDERLAND (A) F.A. CUP 6TH ROUND 1973 0–2.

After the Town's 1–0 league win over Sunderland the previous week, there was a certain amount of confidence as we flew north. (Yes, there was a chartered plane due to the rail strike.) However, the Town was never at the races, and two second half goals from Dave Watson and Ron Guthrie sent most of the 53,151 crowd home happy. Sunderland of course went on to win the cup.

5. v EVERTON F.A. CUP SEMI-FINAL AT VILLA PARK 1985 1–2.

Before the game, I felt that I would not have minded Luton losing unless we were really thrashed, or lost out at the end. The latter was what happened, when Kevin Sheedy's incorrectly-hit free kick crept inside the post four minutes from the end, to equalise Ricky Hill's first half goal. The winner by Dave Watson in extra time was inevitable, and the name of the referee John Martin will live long in the Town supporters' memories.

Eric Morecambe with the Junior Hatters in the '70s. GO

6. v WIMBLEDON F.A. CUP SEMI-FINAL AT WHITE HART LANE 1988 1–2.

Was this the worst semi-final game ever played? Only 25,963 saw Wimbledon kick and scrap (literally) their way to victory over an under par Town side, aided by the worst refereeing performance ever seen from Keith Hackett. (The same referee who had given Dean Saunders two ridiculous penalties in the Littlewoods Cup semi-final at Oxford.) Wimbledon was allowed to do just as they pleased, and even worse they went on to lift the Cup.

Haydn Rudd

I have been a Luton fan since 1967. This was when I first became a season ticket holder. My mother and father are avid Luton supporters.

They saw Joe Payne score ten goals against Bristol Rovers at Kenilworth Road in 1936 – making the result 12–0.

Over the years, myself, mother and father have seen many Luton matches away. We have either travelled by car, or by using the special train service from Luton. Then in 1970 we started using the supporters' coach regularly.

My mother died of cancer at the age of 84. But my father is still as keen as ever, at his present age of 83. In 1967, when I first started following the Town, Luton were fourth from the bottom of Division 4 – leaving four points to spare before being relegated out of the league.

Then over the next few years, Luton Town began to make a success of things again, with promotion to the third division. The following season they went up as champions.

After a year in the third division, Luton won promotion again into Division 2. Then a couple of years later, they finally made it into Division 1.

It seemed unbelievable at the time, that little Luton Town was back playing the likes of Manchester United, Spurs and Liverpool, etc., etc. Although it was great to be there, Luton was relegated at the end of the season, because of the limited resources at the club.

However, good times were not that far away. After a couple of seasons in Division 2, Luton were back on the promotion

Eric Morecambe with the comedy duo, Cannon and Ball. GO

trail again. And in 1982, Luton Town finally made it back into Division 1.

Luton was able to stay in Division 1 for ten years, before being relegated to a new Division 1. Which is not bad going for a club with no money to buy in new players, compared to the richest of Division 1's football teams.

Despite this, Luton has had some very good managers, e.g. Allan Brown, Alec Stock, and Harry Haslem.

Harry was a lovely man. He always had a smile on his face, and a good word for everyone. When Harry moved from Luton to Sheffield United, all at Luton wished him well. When Harry died, his death became a sad day for football, and a great loss to the game. The name Harry Haslem will always linger on within Luton Town F. C. Especially amongst those who had the privilege to have known him. Then came Pleat. He is classed as a very good manager by a lot of Luton supporters. He has a very good eye for a players, as well as doing incredibly well in wheeling and dealing within the transfer market.

When David Pleat left Luton to go to Spurs, then Leicester City, a lot of supporters lost faith in him, because of the way he left the club. When he came back for a second spell at Luton, the club found it hard to gel like it did the first time, so Mr Pleat left again for Sheffield Wednesday.

Luton's other recent managers have been Jimmy Ryan and Terry Westley. Both of these did not seem right for the job. Despite being hard working and nice people, they weren't quite what we needed, and also they found it hard to fit into the club. Then there is Ray Harford. I did not like him as a manager and because of this I rate him as the worst manager Luton has ever seen.

Now to our present manager Lennie Lawrence, who is a very good man for the job at Luton. He has the experience of good football, i.e. he knows how to get players playing their best. Also he is a good tactician and above all, Lennie knows what it is to work with a club with next to no money to spend.

However, in now looking at my memorable experiences in following Luton Town, I find that most of these have been at away games. In one game Luton was playing Portsmouth away. A Luton supporter was stabbed near to the Pompy ground at Fratton Park. After the game had finished and Luton supporters were back at the station, the police would not let any Luton supporters get on the train, or even onto the platform. They were searching everybody and asking a lot of questions regarding the stabbing near to the stadium earlier. Eventually Luton supporters were allowed on the train, with the police joining us to continue the search. But nothing was ever found.

On the train back from Middlesborough away, the engine had broken down at Pontefract station. And within a few minutes, the railway banks were covered in police with their dogs. They told everyone to stay on the train. But some of the young lads did not take any notice of the police and promptly got off the train. They started running up and down the railway bank, with the police and their dogs chasing them around. The young lads began to make fun of the police by making the dogs bark even more. Myself and fellow supporters found this to be very funny and great entertainment. Then about half an hour later, the train started moving again. It was being pushed by another train full of Derby County supporters on their way back from Sunderland. When the trains were due to go their separate ways at Leicester, all the Derby County and Town fans were seen hanging out of the train windows, shouting obscenities to each other, before finally going their separate ways. Which I also found classic football fun!

Then on the way to another away game in Blackpool the train with Luton supporters on it was stopped at Nuneaton station. All the people on the train had to cross over to the other platform, to pick up the train on the other side, because of a fire that occurred further up the line. The train driver driving the train with the Luton supporters now on it, was in a dispute with British Rail over pay. Whilst the dispute was being sorted out, Luton supporters had to wait on the platform before the train could finally leave for Blackpool.

The team was also on this train, and we didn't arrive in Blackpool until 2.55pm. The team who were already changed into their playing kits, ran along the platform to where a coach was waiting to take them to the stadium. The game was played around Christmas time, and there was a parade of Father Christmases with reindeers and little helpers near to the station. So in order for the Town players to get to the ground, the parade was held up, just so the team could make it in time for kick off.

As for the supporters, everyone was dashing around outside the station trying to find taxis. But when we all finally arrived at the stadium, things had to get better. And so they did with a Luton win over Blackpool. Making the result: LUTON 2 BLACKPOOL 0.

On one trip, I saw a carriage table having been thrown out of the window, come flying past my carriage while we were on the way to Hull. Which was quite amazing.

So as you can see, life is never dull in being an away fan, especially when travelling with fellow Luton supporters, irrespective of the result.

Kent Martensson

Luton Town F. C. has many supporters in Sweden. I have supported the Town since they won promotion from Division 3 in the 1969/70 season. But my relationship with the club did not start until the summer of 1972, when I was sent various things from the then club secretary, Bob Readhead.

During the time I have supported the Town, I have made up various diaries recording the ups and downs since 1975. I am a very keen supporter with a lot of information on the club. Yet there was a time in the 1970s when my support for the club dwindled for a few years as an interest in women took over!

But all I hope for now is that Luton will be on the up, as opposed to the down.

Chapter 6

Luton Are The Champions, 1982

It was the season of 1981/82 that saw Luton as the champions of Division 2, after a long struggle. Now we go to the management, players and supporters, who tell of the day we went up, and how we later progressed.

Clive Goodyear

I am Luton Town F. C.'s present physiotherapist. But I began my career as a player for Luton Town in 1978–1984, and had six years with David Pleat.

My best moments as a player were when Luton Town became Division 2 champions, and when beating Man. City in order to stay up.

My worst moment was finishing my career through injury. In 1984 I moved to Plymouth, then in 1987 I signed for Wimbledon. It was after Wimbledon had won the F.A. Cup final against Liverpool in '87, that I found I had damaged cruciate ligaments in my knee. Which now meant that I could no longer play. So I took up physiotherapy instead. I went out to Hong Kong, but when I came back I began looking for a job as a physio. When David Pleat came back to Luton as manager in 1991, he offered me a job part-time. Then a year later, I took over full time.

Being a physio is very different, but I am helpful to the players, in the sense that I know what the players are going through, and they are able to take comfort from that. I really enjoy this job, and I am able to get a lot of pleasure from it when the injured player finally gets better and is back on the pitch playing again. When a player comes to me, I think of ways to cheer him up. And one of them is being able to take the mickey out of him, and vice versa. But it is so boring being injured. I am especially able to encourage the players by getting into their minds.

My dislikes are in the fact that there is not enough money to spend on improving the physio room. In the job as physio you have to work long unsociable hours. But the perks are the trips away and the fact that it is so rewarding.

Brian Stein

I joined Luton Town from Edgware Town in the 1977/78 season. Luton was my first professional club.

My first game was in the F.A. Cup replay at Old Trafford, where we played Man. City. We lost that game by 3–2. But the experience of making my debut at Old Trafford was quite remarkable, as I am a fan of Man. United.

My best moments in playing for Luton were when the Town won the Littlewoods Cup in 1988, and also when they won promotion to the old first division (now the Premier) in 1982. It was a great achievement for all the players and everyone else connected with the club.

My worst moment was when Luton had lost against Wimbledon in the F.A. Cup semi-final in 1988. We lost by 2–1. I felt we did not do ourselves justice that day, and it was a big disappointment after qualifying for the final of the Littlewoods Cup.

Yet I had a great time at Luton. Everyone was really friendly. There was a great comradeship amongst the players. They were a very close-knit family club. The players used to go out every Wednesday, and this had produced great team spirit that was apparent on the pitch.

Whilst I was at Luton, I found the away supporters ban a drawback, because the atmosphere wasn't very good. But I liked playing on the plastic pitch. It improved a lot of the players' technique, in the sense that the plastic pitch highlights the technical problems.

Over the years, I have experienced a few funny moments when playing for Luton Town. One of them was at Christmas

David Pleat holding the Division 2 trophy in 1982. GO

time when all the apprentices had to stand naked in the dressing room with wellington boots on, and sing a song. This made the apprentices feel like one of the family, and it can be seen as an initiation ceremony. You could always have a laugh with everyone. Which probably added to our success.

Finally, I was happy to contribute to so many wins at Luton Town, including winning the Littlewoods Cup in 1988.

Brian Stein and Paul Walsh on international duty in France for England in 1984. GO.

Robert Farnham

I have supported Luton since 1976. During this time I have seen many games both at home and away.

One of my best memories was when Luton played Shrewsbury at home. They had to win this game in order to win the championship of 1982. At half-time Luton were drawing 1–1, but during the second half, Luton scored a further three goals. After the game, people started to pile on to the pitch to join in the celebrations, knowing that Luton were definitely back in DIvision 1.

My worst moment has to be the siege that Luton was under by Millwall supporters in 1985. Brian Stein had scored the goal against them, leaving Millwall to find the equaliser that never came.

Paul Walsh

I played for Luton between the years 1982–84. I have fond and happy memories of Luton. But my best memory of Luton was when we played Man. City. We had to win this game to stay up. With only five full minutes left of the game, it seemed as if Luton was going down. But with only three minutes to go, Raddy Antic scored the only goal of the game. After the whistle had gone, I found it great to see David Pleat skipping across the pitch in excitement.

My other memories of the club were the occasions when I scored five hat tricks against various opposition. Overall my time at the club was great, and I found the club to be very friendly, especially when Luton had just won promotion. It appeared to be a very exciting time for everyone connected with Luton Town F. C.

David Pleat

I first came to Luton in 1978–86, before going to Tottenham Hotspur. Then I came back in 1991–95, before I again left to go to Sheffield Wednesday as their manager.

My hope for Luton Town F. C., before I became manager, was to go forward, though well knowing what the constraints were, and the necessity to work within them.

The main difficulty I had at Luton was they could never capitalise on success. But what inspired me the most as manager was seeing young players such as Hartson, Thomas, Hill, Parker, etc. progress. As well as signing great bargains such as Walsh, Elliot, Donaghy, Moss, Stein, Horton, Nicholas, etc.

Kirk Stevens in goal against Liverpool at Anfield. GO

My best memories of Luton were in promoting exciting football. And my worst memory is the people of Luton not understanding the need for change after eight-and-a-half years and four years.

I was devoted to the job of being Luton's manager, and had a great affinity with the people. I also found Luton to be unique, in the sense of feeling myself to be David fighting Goliath on and off the field.

Graham Mackrell

I worked at Luton Town as club secretary for five years in the '80s. They were very eventful, and I was lucky to be involved with the club at an exciting time in its history.

My best moment at the club has to be the match with Man. City at Maine Road on 14 May 1983. We had found the step up to the first division quite difficult. But until the week before we had looked like struggling through satisfactorily and building for the next season.

Team photograph of players who brought the Division 2 Trophy to Luton in 1982. LN.
Back row: Raddy Antic, Brian Stein, Steve White, Frank Bunn, Clive Goodyear, Jake Findlay, Mike Saxby,
Alan Judge, Pasquale Fuccillo, Paul Keys, Mal Donaghy, Brian Horton, Mark Aizlewood.
Front row: Neil Madden, Rob Johnson, Wayne Turner, Ray Brammer, Godfrey Ingram, Kirk Stephens,
Seamus Heath, Michael Small, Ricky Hill.

Then suddenly on 7 May 1983 we lost 5–1 at home to Everton. This meant that we had to get either a result at Old Trafford on the Monday, (we lost 3–0), or a win at Maine Road on the Saturday and so relegate Man. City.

The day of the game was electric, the journey up the motorway seemed to be a mass of white, orange and blue.

The game itself was too tense to be enjoyable, and despite giving it our best shot it looked as though it would be back to Division 2 next season.

Suddenly with four minutes left, Raddy Antic became our saviour and instantly became a legend when he met Brian Stein's cross to score the only goal of the game. There then followed the longest four minutes of my life. Until the final whistle sparked an incredible contrast.

The Luton fans were ecstatic, the Man. City supporters stood there absolutely numb, unable to absorb the fact that five minutes after thinking themselves safe, they were now relegated.

I don't remember much about the rest of the day, other than

The front cover of the programme against Man. City at Maine Road on May 14th 1983.

to recall that I hardly drank, and was so mentally drained, I was asleep by 11 o'clock.

In stark contrast to that experience is the sixth round F.A. Cup tie versus Millwall at Kenilworth Road on 13 March 1985. Everyone at the club was really excited at the prospect. It was the draw the club wanted, and there was an expectancy that we could be in the semi-finals by the end of the evening. We were, but even the most professional of us gained very little satisfaction.

The conduct of an element of the visiting supporters was a disgrace, and when returning to the ground the following morning to see local residents clearing up their wrecked homes, it was hard not to come to the conclusion that the game of football was suddenly not very important.

My most amusing incident was on a trip with the team to Cyprus. David Pleat and the players had gone ahead, and I flew out a few days later with David Evans and Bill Tomlins. The first day, as we walked down the road, we were passed by Ricky Hill and Brian Stein roaring past on big American easy rider motorbikes, just wearing shorts, no crash helmet or anything. Over a cup of coffee David Evans remonstrated with the manager that there were two very expensive assets of the club, recklessly endangering themselves. David gave a little smile and said, 'Don't look round Mr Chairman or you'll see Steve Foster on a paraglider'.

Chapter 7

Millwall Goes Too Far, 1985

It was in the mid-1980s, that Luton Town F. C. became the innocent victims of one of the most horrendous incidents football has ever seen, at Kenilworth Road during the sixth round F.A. Cup tie against Millwall. This game led to the partial destruction of Luton Town F. C. stadium on March 13 1985. And from this flowed major changes to Kenilworth Road.

In the following news report of March 21st 1985 by Dennis O'Donoghue, he says this about the game:

'The message, "Welcome to the wonderful world of football", flashes up on the electric scoreboard at Kenilworth Road before every match. There was nothing wonderful about Luton Town's ground on Wednesday 13th March 1985, as hundred of Millwall followers ran amok, creating fear and disgust in equal measure for Luton supporters.

'It should have been a night of rejoicing for the town, as Luton reached the semi-finals of the F.A. Cup for the first time in twenty-six years. Instead, the champagne tasted like cider vinegar.

'Luton was given early warning of the trouble to come as Millwall's army descended on the town.

'By 5.00pm windows in pubs and shops in the Castle Street area of the town – including the Phoenix and Castle Street newsagents – had been broken, and police were in pursuit of a gang in Park Street.

'At the ground, the Kenilworth Road terrace reserved for visiting fans was packed by 7pm – forty-five minutes before kick-off – and supporters were already sitting on the scoreboard supports and the passageway cages that divide the terraces into three sections, after turnstiles had been broken down. For one fan, the crush didn't matter at all! He was practically comatose with drink and had to be helped by a St. John ambulanceman.

'At 7.10pm, police and stewards alike were swept aside as hundreds of visiting supporters scaled the fences behind the goal, and raced down the pitch to the Oak Road end. There was no question that they meant quite simply to taunt the Luton fans on the Oak Road. A hail of bottles, cans, nails, 50p and £1 coins sent the home supporters back up the terraces. But they could hardly move because of their number, and the newcomers coming onto the Oak Road from the turnstiles.

'Luton footballers, who came out to warm up in the Oak Road end goalmouth, rapidly disappeared – they would have been better warming up at one of the bonfires started on the Kenilworth Road terrace in any event. The police were powerless to stop the missile throwing, and when one officer tried to intervene, he was set upon.

'For many of the home supporters, enough was enough. The appeals over the loudspeakers for the trouble-makers to return to the Kenilworth Road end were interspersed with messages from Luton fans – fathers separated from sons, mothers from daughters, from husbands and fathers, friends from friends – all with one aim in mind: to get out and get home while they still could.

'The rabble took over the Bobbers stand, ignoring scoreboard messages that the game wouldn't start until they moved. They even disregarded a loud speaker appeal from Millwall manager George Graham, and it wasn't until Mr Graham made a touchline appearance that they vacated their hijacked seats. Even then, many infiltrated the main stand, where isolated fights broke out and some seats were ripped out.

'The arrival of police dogs did much to move the fans, although ironically Millwall defender Lindsey Smith came closest to feeling the sharp teeth of the law. While warming up, he offered his hand to a police dog and hastily snatched it back as a set of canine canines snapped shut!

'Despite the interruptions, the game started practically on

time with many watching it from on top of the Bobbers stand after climbing up the floodlight pylons.

'But the match was only fourteen minutes old when the rowdies came over the fences again, forcing referee David Hutchinson – a police inspector – to take the teams off for twenty-five minutes, during which time he tried a loud speaker appeal.

'When the game did restart – and once Brian Stein had scored – the big fear was that another pitch invasion would be made in order to have the game abandoned if Millwall were still losing.

'A couple of attempts were launched, but extra police, forming a cordon along the triangle end of the main stand, kept control, although some seats were ripped out, causing a head injury to a steward.

'Luton goalkeeper Les Sealey, who had the ordeal of standing at the Millwall end during the second-half, was hit on the head by an object and in addition a knife was also found in the goalmouth! Sealey in fact received early warning from referee Richardson that the final whistle was about to blow, and was practically already in the dressing room when it did.

'One fan made a grab for Luton coach Trevor Hartley who raced out of the dug-out, but fortunately failed to get a secure grip. Within seconds, the hooligans were back on the pitch and in the Bobbers stand tearing out seats, and ripping down fences. These were the scenes which shocked and disgusted the nation, when they were televised, and one can only applaud the BBC's decision to make the film available to the police.

'Even at this point there was a moment of humour. The hero of the night was the police dog who got a good grip on the seat of one fleeing rowdy's trousers, and left him with his backside hanging out.

'Another lad, one pace ahead of a pursuing policeman, jumped over the fence into the main stand, fell and opened up a cut over his eye as he collided with the edge of a seat. He burst into tears, but in truth, there weren't many who felt too much sympathy for him.'

Then in the same issue of the Luton News, Brian Swain the sports editor reports: –DIRECTORS TELL PLAN TO AVOID MORE TROUBLE.'

The aftermath of the Millwall riots. LN

'The second invasion within twenty-four hours was a much more peaceful affair as national and international press gathered at Kenilworth Road while repairs got under way.

'Club executives met for four hours, still shocked by the horror that had spoiled Luton Town's best F.A Cup run since 1959. Chairman David Evans missed the occasion, but was kept in touch with the developments through a stream of phone calls to Singapore, where he was on a business trip.

'Chief Executive John Smith and manager David Pleat, both newly appointed directors, emerged at the end of the private meeting to face a barrage of TV lights, radio reporters and pressmen from a dozen or more news agencies.

'And the Club's handling of press enquiries will stand them in good stead.

'The evidence of the damage done to the Club, to the town and to innocent people was clear enough.

'The TV recording of the trouble made it obvious that the trouble emanated from people pretending to be football supporters from London.

'The press observers took in the message, Luton Town may be open to criticism about crowd control, ticket arrangements, safety facilities and so on. But the fuse that burst into violent flame was brought in and lit by visitors.

'Luton are prepared to put themselves in trouble with the football league by Mr Smith's first announcement at the press conference – rather than subject the town and its football fans to such appalling violence, Luton will simply refuse to play any match likely to produce trouble.

'It is just possible that Luton will be relegated this season, and that Millwall will be promoted, in which case the clubs will be due to meet again in the second division.

'If it happens Luton will refuse to play the game. They will allow Millwall to take all the points by default. They will do it, even if it means the points Luton lose cost them promotion. And even if the Football League imposes a fine, "It's time someone made a stand," said Mr Smith.

'Demands for a ban on the sale of alcohol at grounds will make little difference to Luton Town – and would have made no difference to last week's Millwall hooligans.

'No bars were open at Kenilworth Road. But coaches from

London were pouring into Luton in mid-afternoon on Wednesday, and a lot of them, said Mr Smith, were carrying fans who were already drunk.'

It took five weeks for the directors and executives to decide the future of Kenilworth Road stadium, after the Millwall riots. The proposed plan of the changes to the ground and the club, is reported in the Luton News on April 25th 1985 by Brian Swain, the sports editor:

'This week's announcement that they hope to lay a plastic pitch during the summer is the tip of the iceberg of ideas being considered in the recently-modernised boardroom.

'As well as the following major suggestions that are believed to include:

A new main stand with fewer pillars to obstruct customers' view of the pitch;

A complete rebuilding of the Kenilworth Road terrace, with houses and club offices behind the terrace being demolished to make way for a sports and leisure complex and new offices;

The Kenilworth Road terrace to be roofed over, and turned into the home supporters' area of the ground;

Seats to be installed behind the Oak Road goal;

Executive boxes to replace the Bobbers stand seats;

More social club and sponsor suite facilities to be built in the Hatters Club area.

'And the most radical change, but one which looks ahead many years, is to buy up properties around the ground to enable the pitch to be turned sideways, with the Kenilworth Road end housing the main stand.'

However, at the end of the 1984/85 season, decisions went ahead for a new pitch that is plastic, which is to be used instead of grass. So, what with the new pitch being installed in the summer of 1985, the changes to the stadium were now to take place in the summer of 1986. And these were the changes to the stands.

Yet despite all of this, Luton Town F. C. still has further problems with regard to its ground. And in 1989, the F.A. and other football clubs started to protest about Luton Town's plastic pitch.

David Pleat and David Evans digging up the pitch for the new plastic version. LN

Therefore in a news report by Brian Swain, in the Luton News on July 7 1989, regarding the pitch it says:

'The fight to save the synthetic pitch for league football at Kenilworth Road is likely to put Luton Town at loggerheads with most of the big Football League clubs on Friday.

'At the meeting the League Commission has said the Kenilworth Road pitch has suffered too much use. The Town see proof that it has been successful in giving the community a facility that is not available at places like Anfield and Highbury.

'But they have taken the point, and are going ahead with the provision of a new £60,000 top surface this summer.'

The relaying of the plastic pitch. LN

What with this in mind, Luton Town F. C. replaced their old plastic pitch with a brand new one, in the summer of 1989, which nearly completes the changes following the Millwall riots. But it wasn't until the 1990s that the changes to the ground were completed fully.

Chapter 8

Wembley Heroes, 1988

1988 was the year that every Luton supporter remembers with pride. This was the year that Luton won the League Cup, then known as the Littlewoods Cup.

The previous season, 1986/87, Luton were not allowed to be in it, due to their banning of all away fans. Once the ban was lifted, Luton were now hungry for the Cup.

So in 1988 Luton were back at Wembley, playing in a Cup final. The whole town was looking forward to this game, and a total of 25,000 Luton supporters turned out to see the team play at Wembley. They all dressed in the

Steps at Wembley in the final of the Littlewoods Cup 1988. JP

Some of the thousands of Luton fans in the town centre waiting for the open-top bus to make its way to the Town Hall. JP

official club colours, white, orange and blue. The atmosphere was brilliant.

Luton were playing Arsenal in the final. During the game, Luton scored first, then Arsenal equalised. Still in the first half, Arsenal scored again. Having Dibble in goal proved a Godsend, as he then made an excellent save from a Winterburn penalty.

In the second half, Luton eventually scored the equaliser. Then, with a few minutes left, the winner, making the final result: LUTON 3 ARSENAL 2.

The fans could not believe it, as Steve Foster went to collect the Littlewoods Cup trophy – the first time that Luton had ever won a cup.

On the following Monday, the players on an open-top bus made their traditional way through the noisy, colourful streets of their home town, brandishing the Cup before thousands of delirious fans.

Steve Foster

I played for Luton Town between 1984–1989. Nearly all Luton Town fans will have fond memories of me. My best moment in playing for Luton was being able to pick up the Littlewoods Cup trophy at Wembley in 1988, after beating Arsenal 3–2. This was the greatest day of my whole career as a footballer. My worst moment was leaving, as I liked the club and supporters. But I disliked the negative councillors at Luton, as they would not allow the club to invest in the ground.

I found Ray Harford to be a good coach, but as a manager, he wasn't very good. Yet I enjoyed all of my time at Luton as well as the social life!

David Oldfield

I first joined Luton Town F. C. at the age of thirteen, as a schoolboy. In 1984 I signed from apprentice to professional. Then in 1989, I left Luton for Man. City, before coming back and re-signing for Luton in 1995.

My best memories are winning the Littlewoods Cup in 1988, and winning twice at Goodison Park ages ago. I enjoyed playing in the 1980s for Luton, they were very good years.

I like playing against teams I once used to play for. I have found Luton to be a very friendly club. It was very disappointing for all when we got relegated in 1996.

There is still a lot of talent at Luton. And I find the supporters to be just as passionate about Luton as people are about the big clubs, such as Man. United, Newcastle, etc.

Finally with regards to playing football, I find there is a lot of frustrating time-wasting that goes on, when a player gets knocked down in a tackle.

Julian James

I have been a footballer at Luton since 1986. I joined Luton at the age of fourteen as a schoolboy, before signing as an apprentice at sixteen.

My best moment was the first time I came on the pitch as a Luton player. It was in a first team game against Southampton away. I made a full debut in the 1987/88 season. This game resulted in a 1–1 draw.

I immensely enjoyed the Wembley trips of 1988 against Arsenal, 1989 against Nottingham Forest, and in 1994 against Chelsea.

I like the way football is played at Luton. But I dislike being moved about to play in so many different positions.

Since my time at Luton, there have been a couple of funny incidents on the pitch. The first one was when Marvin Johnson for no reason just fell over. When talking with him, he reckoned that someone had tackled him from behind. But they never did.

And the second one was when Luton played Tottenham Hotspur away. One of the Luton players decided to put a bet on who would have the first throw in of the game, us or them. When Luton was out on the pitch, both teams would not dare to kick the ball out of play. But eventually a Luton player got fed up, and kicked the ball out of play, when he had a lot of space around him to score. Everyone could not believe it, especially the bench. But when they later found out what went on, they could see the funny side of it.

Whilst I've been at Luton, I have endured seven operations. I find injuries a nightmare, and having to go into hospitals, as I totally hate them.

Mick Harford

I played for Luton Town between the years 1984–1990. Then I had a spell at Derby County, before re-joining Luton again in 1991–1992. My experiences in playing for Luton are mainly of happy ones, and probably the most enjoyable of my whole career. I joined a team languishing at the foot of the old first division. But I had the opportunity of playing with some of Luton's best players, i.e. Brian Stein, Steve Foster, Ricky HIll, etc., who turned Luton into a very good footballing team, surely creating the ability to win major honours.

Obviously my best moment was winning the Littlewoods Cup, which I think is the favourite memory of everyone connected with the club during this period.

My other great memory was being able to play for England whilst a Luton player. My worst moments in playing for Luton were obtaining injuries and having to miss games.

Yet my biggest disappointment has to be when Luton weren't allowed to play in Europe after winning the Littlewoods Cup. This can be seen as a great minus for players, supporters and the club alike.

Mike Newell

I played for Luton Town between the years 1986–87, being able to play in every league and cup game in that season, which was when Luton finished seventh in the league (old Division 1).

My best moments in playing for Luton include scoring a hat trick against Liverpool in October 1986, where the result was 4–1. Then again in the second replay of the F.A. Cup 3rd round in January 1987, when Luton won 3–0 against Liverpool.

In looking at my worst memories, these have to be when we lost to Q.P.R. a week later. As well as the uncomfortable feelings I had when at the club, as I did not like the artificial pitch nor the ban on away supporters.

But overall I have good memories of Luton and enjoyed playing for them.

This is the team photograph of the players who played in the centenary year of 1985, and also many of this squad went on to play in the Littlewoods Cup final in 1988. GO

Back row: Mark Stein, Rob Johnson, Ricky McEvoy, Stacey North, Marc North, Ray Daniel, David Preece, Marcus Tuite.

Second row: John Moore (Coach), Emeka Nwajiobi, Tim Breacker, Les Sealey, Paul Elliott, Andy Dibble, Mick Harford, Mitchell Thomas, John Faulkner (Coach).

Third row: Trevor Hartley (Ass. Manager), Gary Parker, Ricky Hill, Mal Donaghy, Steve Foster, David Pleat (Manager), Peter Nicholas, Ashley Grimes, John Sheridan (Physio.).

Front row: David Oldfield, Ian Scott, Gary Cobb, John Kennedy, Aaron Tighe, Richard Harvey, Paul Lewis, Matthew Bowden, Duncan Berry, Marvin Johnson, Sean Farrell.

Luton players parading around Wembley with the Littlewoods Cup Trophy in 1988. SK Mal Donaghy, Mark Stein, Andy Dibble, Danny Wilson, Ashley Grimes, Rob Johnson, David Preece (hidden), Mick Harford.

Les Sealey

I played for Luton between 1983–1990. My worst memory came when Luton lost 3–1 in the final of the League Cup game against Nottingham Forest in 1989.

Thomas Moller

I am only one of the ninety or so supporters that follow the Hatters from Norway. I have supported the Town since they won promotion in 1982, as I wanted to support a smaller club in England.

My best moment in following the Hatters has to be when Luton was at Wembley, on 24 April 1988 against Arsenal for the Cup. I found this to be a tremendous occasion, as I was able to attend this game at Wembley. But what's even more amazing, it was the first Town match that I have ever seen in England.

My worst moment was when Luton Town played away at Meadow Lane on May 2nd 1992. It was a very sad day, except that the build-up to the match was fantastic. I was able to meet Raddy Antic outside the arena, and told Raddy what I thought of his contribution at Maine Road in 1983. During this game at Meadow Lane, Luton Town scored first against Notts. County – but ended up relegated. All thanks to Rob Mathews.

For the supporters' club in Norway, David Pleat gave me Luton Town's complete away kits after the 1991/1992 season. The supporters of Luton Town use these kits annually in a big supporters' tournament in Norway. There are as many as thirty-six clubs who compete against each other in Oslo. In 1993, Luton Town supporters club beat Man. United supporters club. The Man. United and Liverpool supporters' clubs have over 12,000 each in Norway. In all, there are sixty different supporters' clubs in Norway that support English soccer, and who follow English teams.

Iain Dowie

I played for Luton Town F. C. between 1987–1991. My best memory was when the Town played Crystal Palace in the second to last game of the season. In the 90th minute Jason

Preece crossed the ball for me to score the only goal of the game. Had we lost this game, we would have been relegated to Division 2 after the Derby County game the following week.

However, my worst moment was not being used as a sub. in the Littlewoods Cup final against Arsenal in 1988 because I had just joined Luton. I felt that I was playing well enough to be included.

I liked my time at Luton; it is a family club, and I felt that I had made the right choice of club, ensuring a good start to my football career. I was able to work with good players and I learned a lot from them.

I don't have any real dislikes, except the stadium. Yet the pitch was nice to play on. And whilst I was there, I found there was always a regular crowd of hard-core supporters that came to watch Luton play.

Regular Luton fans travel down to Torquay in the first round of the F. A. Cup. AH

I had a fantastic time at Luton, and I will always appreciate the start it gave me.

Wayne Turner

I was born in Luton, and I signed for Luton schoolboys when I was just fourteen. Then at sixteen, I signed as apprentice before turning professional at seventeen.

I had ten years as a player, playing for Luton, Brentford, and Barnet. At Barnet I got to be a player coach, then eventually coach. Then one day, David Pleat came to ask me for my services as a reserve team coach at Luton Town F. C. Having agreed, I was reserve team coach until Lennie Lawrence came. Then Lennie made me first team coach, a job that I'm doing now – the highlight of my career. I have had some good memories of Luton, and my biggest one has to be at the age of sixteen. When I was offered a job as a painter and decorator, David Pleat said, 'Don't take it, as you will be an apprentice soon'. So I took his advice and gave professional football a chance.

Another big memory was making my first team debut against Wrexham, where we lost 2–0, but I still remember it with great affection. Other great memories are the cup runs of 1985, and scoring the winning goal in the 3rd round replay against Watford.

My worst memories are losing the semi-final of the F.A. Cup against Everton by 2–1, and relegation in 1996 was devastating.

I have been subject to many a funny story in professional football. But one of them was when I played in my second first team game at eighteen for Luton against Bristol Rovers. I was marking a very good winger at the time, so Paul Price said, 'Get a good tackle on him and you won't be booked'. So what did the referee do? He booked me for following Mr Price's advice. Paul Price was laughing when it happened, and at half-time he said, 'Don't believe anything that I say'. Then in the second half, the right winger gave me a pasting, and because of what happened I dared not do anything else wrong. This seems to have affected me as a young boy.

But I like the style of football that is played at Luton. I get great enjoyment from the way we play, and from the goals that we score in using that style of play.

Yet what I dislike the most is the uncertainty of the club, and the fact that every decision made is short-term.

Luton Town 3 Arsenal 2

BRILLIANT!

Thousands turn out to greet their Wembley heroes

WELL DONE you Hatters!

That was the cry from 20,000 happy fans as Steve Foster (right) and the boys of Luton Town came home with the cup.

George Street was a sea of straw boaters and orange and blue favours as the team paraded the Littlewoods Challenge Trophy on the Town Hall balcony on Monday.

Their fans, including toddlers and pensioners, were in raptures. Some described it as the most euphoric night since the end of World War Two.

● INSIDE this week — a 16-page supplement on the Hatters' Wembley wonder starts on page 23.

The front page of the Luton News that shows the fans celebrating after the 3–2 win at Wembley against Arsenal.

69

My aspiration for the next few years is to improve the youth policy and to push through young players. As they can ensure the club's survival.

My time at Luton Town is very enjoyable, especially since being made first team coach, as I am able to decide my own destiny, day and night, and I am in charge of my own life. I also find the job very rewarding and pleasing. I learned a lot under David Pleat and this has helped me get where I am now.

The players and the coaches want to do very well for the club. And there is a determination within the club at present to see that we succeed. So when we lose, it makes it very disappointing for all.

The downside to our smallness is that we have to sell our players in order to survive. Until this changes, there will always be disruptions to the team. We need to become financially secure, and a new stadium could do this for us.

Chapter 9

Changes Complete

The aftermath of the Millwall riots had brought about major changes to Luton Town F. C., and to the Kenilworth Road stadium. In 1990 Luton Town made plans to add more seats to its stadium. An article on May 2 1990 in the Luton News says:

'The installation of 2,000 seats at the front of the Kenilworth Road terrace will displease many fans, but the club says it has little choice but to comply with the recommendations of the Taylor report after Hillsborough, and backed by U.E.F.A.'s demand for all grounds to be all seater by 1994.

'The seats will run the full width of the pitch, so segregation of visiting fans for cup ties becomes even more difficult. So the Oak Stand seats will become the away end for cup games. Season ticket holders in that section will have to move out for cup-ties.'

Now it seems that the supporters at Luton Town F. C. are not happy with the new seating arrangements. As in the Luton News on 6th June 1990. Eric Norris reports:

'FOOTBALL HAS NO CHOICE OVER SEATS'.

'Luton Town season ticket holders who moved from the Bobbers stand, when it was converted into executive boxes, are now upset to learn that their new seats in the Oak Road stand will not be guaranteed for cup-ties next season.

'The town must allow away supporters into the ground for cup games and they will be given the seats behind the Oak Road goal.

'But the Town's general manager, Bill Tomlinson, said the club understood the supporters' feelings, but was in a position where they could do nothing about it.

'He said the decision followed Mr Justice Taylor's report on the Hillsborough disaster, that says in the next five years every ground in the country must be all seats.

'"We have no choice and the plan is to reduce standing by 20% over each of the next five years." We have to have segregation for cup-ties, when we must allow away fans in. Oak Road will be the segregated section for the cup matches. It is the only area of the ground, where we can ensure that the two sets of supporters arrive at different parts of the ground.

POLICE ARE IN FAVOUR

The police want us to do it this way, and it has been under discussion for several years. The Wing Stand has been suggested, but experience has proved it to be unsuccessful, after incidents of trouble when Bristol Rovers came for a cup-tie.

'"Two sets of opposing supporters are only one aisle apart in the Wing Stand."

'He said the Oak Road season tickets would not include cup-tie entitlements. But there is a promise that season ticket holders will have priority to buy tickets in the Main Stand for cup-ties. He emphasised that the change from standing to seats was being forced for football fans, who in general don't want it.

'The seats at the Kenilworth Road end will be introduced over the next five years, and 2,500 will be done in time for next season.'

Following this article in the Luton News, the new stand gets the go-ahead. The plastic pitch gets withdrawn and at the same time the new stand is built in the summer of 1991. And the away supporters are put in the Oak Road Stand.

Which now concludes the fundamental alterations at Kenilworth Road. Since then there has been relatively little change.

In the Luton News of 21st August 1991, the sports editor Brian Swain reports:

'£1 MILLION REFURBISHMENT FOR THE NEW SEASON'

'The impressive results of spending around £1 million during the summer at Kenilworth Road, will be revealed to the customers for the visit of Liverpool and some of their fans on

Saturday. The Football Ground Improvements Trust paid three-quarters of the bill. The stadium has been transformed, with the most eye-catching addition the new 714-seat stand on the old triangle.

'It has filled in the last remaining open space, and suddenly Kenilworth Road looks to me like the sort of ground a club could live in happily for years to come, particularly if re-development can one day go ahead on the lego-land site, which used to house the Bobbers stand.

Here are Luton supporters in the newly built executive boxes. GO

'On the lower steps of the Kenilworth Road end, new seats have been installed to match those behind the other goal, and there has been a solid demand for them.

'The view from the new stand is easily the best in the ground. From most of it you can easily see both goals, with no pillars to hide vital areas.

'One obstruction remains, a floodlight pylon. A slim-line replacement is on order, and due to be installed within a couple of months. Managing director David Kohler bristled when I said the transformation was so impressive that it made me wonder if the club would ever leave.

'He says the work done this summer has no effect on the need to relocate, particularly with the Premier League in the offing. Negotiations to secure a site are still going on, but he felt that in the meantime, the club owed it to its supporters to improve facilities. He added that he was still not satisfied with the Main Stand.

'A new police control box has been built beside the Oak Road end, where up to 2,000 away fans will be seated this season. Six closed-circuit TV cameras, with high-powered lenses and hooked up to video recorders which can provide court evidence, can peer closely at every part of the ground, and at the streets nearby . . .

'The net effect of the changes is that the Town's capacity is down 300 to 13,400 including 9,050 seats. The legal requirement to make it an all seater stadium by 1994, will cut the total to about 11,200. When that happens, ground relocation or a major extension will be a must if the Town are to be in Premier League contention.'

At the moment, Luton town councillors and the chairman David Kohler are discussing moves to another location within Luton. The results of this will not be known until the end of 1997 at the earliest. But at present, it looks promising that by the years 2000, Luton Town F. C. will be re-housed in a new up-to-date all seater stadium. With such a new stadium, we should be able to stay in the Premier League – when Luton Town finally gets there again in the future!

Chapter 10

Life In The '90s

In the present decade Luton has so far suffered relegation twice. Yet whilst we make our way to being a great football team again, we take up the story we started at the very beginning of this book.

David Kohler

I am the Chairman of Luton Town F. C. I became Chairman of Luton in 1991, which came about by buying the majority of shares in the company.

My best memory of Luton so far is beating both Newcastle and West Ham in the cup run of 1994.

My worst memory is relegation.

I have encountered many funny stories during my time as Luton's chairman. One of these is: A good friend left me a message, and said he was Graham Taylor. I then phoned Graham back, thinking he had called up as England manager. Without realising until later that this call was a spoof.

A proud moment that happened at Luton was when the Prime Minister came to watch a game. It was against Chelsea at home in the Christmas of 1992. Luton won by 2–0 with Richard Harvey being one of the scorers.

However, what we need now is a new stadium, because, if we can get a new stadium, then Luton will be on the up. But if not, then there is a possibility that we will be staying were we are. The new stadium is still in public enquiry, and there will not be a result on it until the end of 1997. But we are forever hopeful.

Kathy Leather

I am the marketing director of Luton Town F. C. I've been in this job since 1993 as successor to Andy King. It has opened my eyes to people in football. Before, I couldn't understand the passion that is in a football club until I started working for Luton Town F. C.

The marketing department is involved with supporters' clubs to find out what they want, and what they are happy or not happy with. The supporters care about things commercially and they like to get involved. People seem to underestimate what the supporters do, by getting involved with functions, to bring more money into the club. Which I have found to be absolutely brilliant, but not all other clubs get their supporters involved like Luton does.

Martin, an avid Luton fan, holds the monster scarf for the Town programme. AH

Here are the Luton players of the 1995/96 season at the Junior Hatters Club in Luton. AH

Luton Town has a good education programme, with meetings on Tuesday and Thursday evenings in which local children around Luton can learn what goes on in a football club: and it also helps them to support the club as its local professional club in the future.

My best moment has been simply to be given the opportunity to work at Luton Town F. C. And sitting in the royal box at Wembley in the 1994 semi-final against Chelsea, where Luton lost 2–0. My worst moment was relegation, and it has been hard going since it happened. I like all the supporters and customers connected with the club. But I'm not looking forward to the day we have to start moving out . . . if ever.

Lennie Lawrence

I became Luton Town's manager in December 1995 following Terry Westley's departure. My ambition for the club before I arrived was to remain in the first division. I have encountered a couple of major difficulties whilst managing Luton Town, and these are: a difficulty in reducing the squad size, and consequently bringing in suitable new players.

The thing that has inspired me the most is the support from fans in difficult circumstances. The best memory I have of Luton so far was the away win at Norwich in January 1995, and against Crewe

Lennie Lawrence is all smiles after an away win. AH

at home in December 1996.

My hope for the future is that Luton will be promoted and will be a great team again.

Since arriving at Luton Town F. C. as the manager, I have not found it easy. But I am enjoying every minute of it.

Wayne Turner, Lennie Lawrence and Clive Goodyear watching a game. GO

Trevor Peake

I have been the reserve team coach since the start of 1996, when Lennie Lawrence came as Luton's manager. Wayne Turner was promoted from reserve team coach to assistant manager to the first team. And this was when Lennie Lawrence approached myself to be the coach for the reserve team.

Since then my most special memory is beating Arsenal at Highbury 2–1. And with a lot of youth team players used against Southampton's first team players Luton won 1–0. Which was very good, as it highlights the amount of young talent that we have at Luton Town F. C.

My worst moment was playing against Brighton, where the reserve team players did not play to their full potential, despite winning 2–0.

My dislikes are relegation, as I feel that I am responsible for it to have happened. So it's now my main ambition to put it right. Yet I would like to be around when we return to better days again.

I like the fact that Luton is a homely club, as it allows people to feel at home quite quickly. Mainly because of the people around the town, who made it quite easy for me to settle here.

Gary Waddock

I joined Luton Town from Bristol Rovers at the start of the 1994/95 season. My best memories are: the day I signed for Luton, and making my full debut against Bolton Wanderers, despite losing 2–1.

My worst moment was relegation at the end of the 1995/96 season. I like winning games, and dislike losing games, along with injuries. I have found Luton Town F. C. to be a very friendly club.

Steve Thompson

I played for Luton Town F. C. in the season of 1993/94 for five-and-a-half weeks.. My best memory of Luton was being able to make my debut with Mick Harford. We played Oldham, and Luton beat them 2–1.

My worst memory was having to leave the club, as I liked playing for Luton Town F. C.

Ian Feuer

I joined Luton Town in the November of 1995 from West Ham. My best moment was when I denied Watford a penalty in a game that resulted in a 1–1 draw away on 24 November 1995.

I found the reception that I received from Luton supporters at Barnsley was brilliant. And being nominated player of the year in 1996 just equally as good.

My worst moment was relegation.

However, I have really enjoyed playing for Luton Town. I find the club to be a very friendly club. And despite being relegated, I am still enjoying being a Luton player.

Dwight Marshall, Ian Feuer and Gary Waddock holding their player of the year trophies at a presentation evening held by the Luton Town F. C. Supporters Club. GO

Ian Feuer is seen giving Ceri Hughes some friendly advice. GO

Chris Kamara

I played for Luton Town F. C. between the years 1992–93. My memories of playing for Luton are not very happy ones. Whilst playing for Luton Town, my worst moment was during the game against Grimsby. I did not play at all well, and I presume the crowd thought I was not trying. It was the only time during my long career that I was booed by my own club supporters. Which if I look back I probably deserved.

My best moment in playing for Luton was when we thrashed Arsenal in the old first division, on Boxing Day. It was awful playing away games for Luton during my first season with the club. Simply because we did not win one game away from home.

This climaxed in playing Notts. County (already relegated) on the last day of the season. We were winning 1–0 at half-time, but we lost 2–1 in the end. It was terrible to hear that Coventry had lost to Aston Villa. If the score had remained at 1–0, then we would have stayed up.

I do not consider my time at Luton to have been very good. It is the only club I have been with where I did not win over the supporters. Although having said that, David Pleat and many others always treated me well.

Damien Mathew

I came to Luton Town for one month in 1992 on loan. My best moment in playing for Luton was after a rare piece of dribbling against Bristol City – I hit the post. Then in another game against Derby County, I nearly scored a goal with an overhead kick.

My worst moment was in another game against Bristol City. I went up for a header, and on landing I jarred my back, which then went into spasm. I was able to carry on for about two minutes more – before deciding to come off due to the pain in my back.

I generally enjoyed playing away games for Luton, as there was a good atmosphere from the supporters, which definitely raises a player's game.

Alan Harper

I played for Luton Town between 1993–94. My worst moment whilst playing for Luton was when we were beaten by Chelsea in the semi-final of the F.A. Cup at Wembley. (We did not do ourselves justice on the day.)

Probably my best moment was the run up to the semi-final. We played very well, and we should have gone on to the final with a bit of luck.

The funniest moment was in one of my first games for Luton. We played Middlesborough away and were playing very well on this day. I received the ball from Trevor Peake, and then passed it on to Marvin Johnson. He went to control the ball. (I was only five yards away from him at the time.) He missed the ball, ran after it, fell over the ball, and the ball ran out of play. He hurt his ankle and could not stop laughing. When I turned round the whole team was laughing too.

Rob Mathews

I signed from Notts. County to Luton Town in 1995, and left to join York City in the same year. My best moment in playing for Luton was when I made my debut against Port Vale at home in February 1995. Luton lost that game 2–1.

My worst experience was having lots of small injuries. Whilst I was at Luton, I only ever played six away games and started one home game – which was my debut. I was never fit to play more than one home game due to the injuries that had occurred whilst playing away for Luton!

I liked my time at Luton and I found it to be a very friendly club. On match days I found the club to be very helpful towards players' guests, and they made them feel very welcome.

I disliked the way Luton never gave me the opportunity to express myself on the pitch at the start of the 1995/96 season under Terry Westley – when Luton appeared to be struggling in Division 1.

I found the supporters to be really committed to the club, and this made the atmosphere special for everyone playing at Luton Town F. C.

I enjoyed being a Luton player under David Pleat, and found him to be a very knowledgeable man, as well as an experienced man. This made David the best manager I have had the pleasure of working with, because of the skills that he had brought to the game.

Chapter 11

Luton's Near Miss in '97

Having faced the prospect of doom and gloom over the last five years, myself along with other recent supporters never thought the day would come where we would see Luton winning a place in the play-offs for promotion into the first division. Yet it hasn't been very easy, as at the start of our campaign in Division 2 1996, we lost three out of four games. And it all seemed as if this was going to be a repeat of the previous season. But after putting a series of unbeaten runs together we soon proved the country wrong by taking the number two spot in the table most of the season. This would have ensured us an automatic place into Division 1 next season 1997/98. But towards the end of the season some of the games went against us for an automatic promotion spot. We were assured a play-off place, but unfortunately we lost 3–4 on aggregate at the semi-final stage of the play-offs to Crewe Alexandra.

So what contributed to our relative success? Well we all know that success is able to breed success. Yet it wasn't just the first team that was successful, our youth team was as well. They came top in the South East Counties League Division 2, and played extremely well in the F.A. Youth Cup by reaching the semi-finals for the first time in its history. This season 1996/97 saw Luton beat very good footballing sides by very good results, such as 5–1 against Preston North End and Crewe Alexandra 6–0.

Luton also was the envy of the country through Tony Thorpe leading the goal table in Division 2. Which hasn't happened to Luton in a very long time. As well Luton came top in the country's fair play league.

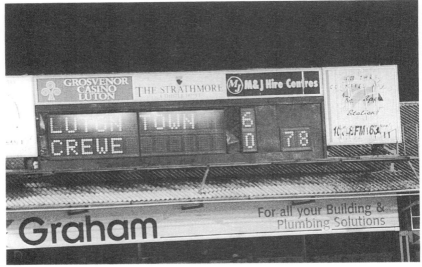

A picture of the score board that shows the time of the sixth goal Luton scored. AH

Tony Thorpe is seen skipping across the goal after completing his hat trick against Crewe Alexandra. AH

Paul Showler

I came to Luton from Bradford City in the summer of 1996. When this season first started I thought that the squad of players was the best I had played with and that we should have a good chance of promotion. Then we lost the first three games! My worst game this season was against Watford at home. I had the worst game of my career. Nothing I did went right.

The best game of the season was when I scored two goals against Peterborough at home. Everything I did that day worked.

My outlook for the future is to have a good season again in division two (1997/98). Since I came to Luton I have found it a very good place to play.

Graham Alexander

I came to Luton from Scunthorpe in the summer of 1995. When this season first started my thoughts were on promotion back into the first division, as I have played in the lower divisions long enough.

My worst game this season was when we lost to Brentford away 3–2 at the start of the season. I wasn't playing too well and got dropped from the Bristol City game that followed, away.

My best game was against Crewe Alexandra when we won 6–0. I was able to set up a few of the goals as well as scoring my first goal of the season.

My hope for the future is to play in Division 1 with Luton. But generally I would like to make it big with regards to football, and to be able to play at an international level.

Some of the most enjoyable moments of the season are in the dressing room before the game. Whilst we are getting ready we play music. Marvin Johnson and Mitchell Thomas always dance to the music in a really funny sort of way by making shapes.

Graham Alexander and David Oldfield celebrating after scoring against Crewe.. AH

Dwight Marshall

I came to Luton from Plymouth Argyle in 1994. When the 1996/7 season first started all I could think about was getting fit again to play in the first team, following my injury after the Sunderland away game in February 1996, which kept me out of the rest of the '95/96 season. Then secondly I wanted to help Luton win promotion back into the first division.

My worst game this season was against Wrexham. I had a chance to score but missed. Yet my best game was when we beat Crewe Alexandra 6–0.

My ambition for the future is for the team to play to a high standard in the first division and to continue where I am in my career at that level with Luton.

Aaron Skelton

I came through the youth system at Luton. At the start of the season my thoughts were to get fit from injury as soon as possible. Then make it into the first team.

My worst game was against Elstree and Borehamwood in the second round of the F.A. Cup. It was a bad game as nothing went right for me, despite winning 2–1.

My best game was against Bournemouth, as I played really well with very few problems.

Steve Davis

I came to Luton from Burnley in 1995. My aim at the start of the season was to get Luton straight back up into Division 1.

Steve Davis signing his autograph for the Junior Hatters at Kenilworth Road. AH

The weakest game for me this season was when we lost 5–0 to Bristol City away, and my best game this season was when we beat Burnley 2–0. It was great to be able to win against my old club at Burnley, and it was nice to see the team being able to keep a clean sheet.

My vision for the future is to see Luton hold our own in the first division, when we get there automatically next season (1997/98)!

Andrew Fotiadis

I came through the youth system at Luton. At the start of the season I was trying to break into the first team regularly, as well as thinking this would be our best chance to bounce straight back up into Division 1.

My worst game of the season was when I made my debut against Burnley at home in the first game of the season. I didn't play well, neither did the team, as we lost 2–1. Also what with this being my first ever league match with the first team, I wasn't used to the pressure of the crowd. Which in some ways seemed to have an affect on my game.

The best game was against Gillingham when I won the man of the match award. My intention is to get Luton promoted and to play in the Premier League with Luton.

Ceri Hughes

The poorest game of the season for me was when we lost to Chesterfield at home by 1–0. The best game of the season was Millwall away when I scored a winner that sent Luton to the top of the table, and the game against

Ceri Hughes and Tony Thorpe celebrating the goal that sent us top of the league, after scoring against Millwall, away. AH

Brentford at home when we won 1–0 to send us back to the top of the league.

My ambition is to make as much money as possible, have children and be healthy.

Kim Grant

I came to Luton Town F. C. from Charlton Athletic in 1996, towards the end of the '95/96 season. My aim at the start of the season was to get promoted and to play more games than I did, as well as trying to become Luton's top scorer. With regards to my worst games, I find it hard to recall any, as I've only played in fourteen games.

My best game this season was against Derby County away, as I was able to score and I played really well in this game.

My hope is to get back into the first team and start playing again in the second division with Luton in 1997/98 season, with myself as Luton's top goal scorer when we win automatic promotion.

Luton fans at Wimbledon, away, after beating Derby County in the second round of the Coca-Cola Cup. AH

David Oldfield

My worst games this season were, (1) Bristol City away, we lost 5–0, and (2) Chesterfield at home when we lost 1–0. They were both bad games and I didn't really enjoy playing in them.

My best game was against Preston North End at home. It was a great win 5–1, and I was able to score my first hat-trick of the season. Next season I am looking for an instant place in the first division by Easter.

Marvin Johnson

I came through the youth system at Luton Town F. C. My intention at the start of the season was to try and adapt to the way most of the teams in the second division play, and hopefully everything should fall into place nicely.

My least enjoyable game this season was against Burnley at home. I did not feel comfortable and was unsure for most of the game. My best game was against Crewe Alexandra away. I enjoyed this game the most because they also try to play football in the way that I like to see the game played.

Like the rest of the team I expect to win promotion again with the Town.

Luton fans look on as Marvin receives treatment at Bolton, away. AH

Chapter 12

Summary

Over the years, Luton's supporters, players, and officials have not only been loyal, but jovial, with a great sense of humour, whether losing or winning games.

Many players have passed through the gates of Luton, some successful, some not. But they all testify to the friendliness of the club, and look back with affection and pride on their time there. The supporters who have travelled in all weathers to follow and support the team, are the backbone of the Club.

Over 4,000 Luton fans travel to make the local derby against Watford at Vicarage Road. AH

Without them, the Club would not exist, nor others like it across the country.

And the chairmen, managers and coaches have played their crucial parts in the complex web that is a dynamic football club, beset by ever-changing fortunes, captivating thousands and holding them in a compulsive, inescapable grip.

Bibliography

Collings T.: LUTON TOWN: A PICTORIAL CELEBRATION OF THEIR HISTORY, *Luton Town F. C. Ltd 1988*

Keith Hayward: MAD AS A HATTER, *Fanzine 1995–1997*

LUTON NEWS:: Home Counties Newspaper plc

PHOTOGRAPHS: Luton News, c/o Luton Museum (LN), Andy Hanley (AH), John Pyper (JP), Gareth Owen (GO), and Stewart Kendall (SK), of Sports Photo Ltd.

Acknowledgements

I would like to express my thanks to the players, supporters and officials at Luton Town F. C. for the help I have received in writing and compiling this book. Special thanks to Simon Oxley, Luton Town's publicity officer, and to the various photographers for generously allowing me the use of their pictures.

Books Published by
THE BOOK CASTLE

JOURNEYS INTO BEDFORDSHIRE: Anthony Mackay.
Foreword by The Marquess of Tavistock, Woburn Abbey.
A lavish book of over 150 evocative ink drawings.

A PILGRIMAGE IN HERTFORDSHIRE: H. M. Alderman.
Classic, between-the-wars tour round the county, embellished
with line drawings.

**COUNTRYSIDE CYCLING IN BEDFORDSHIRE,
Buckinghamshire And Hertfordshire**: Mick Payne.
Twenty rides on- and off-road for all the family.

**PUB WALKS FROM COUNTRY STATIONS:
Bedfordshire and Hertfordshire**: Clive Higgs.
Fourteen circular country rambles, each starting and finishing
at a railway station and incorporating a pub-stop at a mid-way
point.

LOCAL WALKS: South Bedfordshire and North Chilterns:
Vaughan Basham. Twenty-seven thematic circular walks.

LOCAL WALKS: North and Mid-Bedfordshire:
Vaughan Basham. Twenty-five thematic circular walks.

FAMILY WALKS: Chilterns South: Nick Moon.
Thirty 3 to 5 mile circular walks.

**CHILTERN WALKS: Hertfordshire, Bedfordshire and
North Buckinghamshire**: Nick Moon.
CHILTERN WALKS: Buckinghamshire: Nick Moon.
**CHILTERN WALKS: Oxfordshire and
West Buckinghamshire**: Nick Moon.
A trilogy of circular walks, in association with the Chiltern
Society. Each volume contains thirty circular walks.

**OXFORDSHIRE WALKS:
Oxford, the Cotswolds and the Cherwell Valley**: Nick Moon.
**OXFORDSHIRE WALKS:
Oxford, the Downs and the Thames Valley**: Nick Moon.
Two volumes that complement Chiltern Walks: Oxfordshire
and complete coverage of the county, in association with the
Oxford Fieldpaths Society. Thirty circular walks in each.

FOLK: Characters and Events in the History of Bedfordshire and Northamptonshire: Vivienne Evans. Anthology about people of yesteryear – arranged alphabetically by village or town.

LEGACIES:
Tales and Legends of Bedfordshire and Hertfordshire:
Vic Lea. Twenty-five mysteries and stories based on fact, including Luton Town Football Club. Many photographs.

HISTORIC FIGURES IN THE BUCKINGHAMSHIRE LANDSCAPE: John Houghton.
Major personalities and events that have shaped the county's past, including a special section on Bletchley Park.

MANORS and MAYHEM, PAUPERS and POLITICS:
Tales from Four Shires: Beds., Bucks., Herts., and Northants.: John Houghton.
Little-known historical snippets and stories.

MYTHS and WITCHES, PEOPLE and POLITICS:
Tales from Four Shires: Bucks., Beds., Herts., and Northants.: John Houghton.
Anthology of strange but true historical events.

ECCENTRICS and VILLAINS, HAUNTINGS and HEROES:
Tales from Four Shires: Northants., Beds., Bucks., and Herts.: John Houghton.
True incidents and curious events covering one thousand years.

DUNSTABLE WITH THE PRIORY, 1100–1550: Vivienne Evans.
Dramatic growth of Henry I's important new town around a major crossroads.

DUNSTABLE DECADE: THE EIGHTIES:
A Collection of Photographs: Pat Lovering.
A souvenir book of nearly 300 pictures of people and events in the 1980s.

DUNSTABLE IN DETAIL: Nigel Benson.
A hundred of the town's buildings and features, plus town trail map.

OLD DUNSTABLE: Bill Twaddle.
A new edition of this collection of early photographs.

THE RAILWAY AGE IN BEDFORDSHIRE: Fred Cockman.
Classic, illustrated acount of early railway history.

CHILTERN ARCHAEOLOGY: RECENT WORK:
A Handbook for the Next Decade: edited by Robin Holgate.
The latest views, results and excavations by twenty-three leading archaeologists throughout the Chilterns.

WHIPSNADE WILD ANIMAL PARK: 'MY AFRICA': Lucy Pendar.
Foreword by Andrew Forbes. Introduction by Gerald Durrell.
Inside story of sixty years of the Park's animals and people – full of anecdotes, photographs and drawings.

BOURNE and BRED:
A Dunstable Boyhood Between the Wars: Colin Bourne.
An elegantly written, well-illustrated book capturing the spirit of the town over fifty years ago.

ROYAL HOUGHTON: Pat Lovering.
Illustrated history of Houghton Regis from the earliest times to the present.

BEDFORDSHIRE'S YESTERYEARS Vol. 1:
The Family, Childhood and Schooldays:
Brenda Fraser-Newstead.
Unusual early 20th century reminiscences, with private photographs.

BEDFORDSHIRE'S YESTERYEARS Vol. 2:
The Rural Scene: Brenda Fraser-Newstead.
Vivid first-hand accounts of country life two or three generations ago.

BEDFORDSHIRE'S YESTERYEARS Vol. 3:
Craftsmen and Trades People:
Brenda Fraser-Newstead.
Fascinating recollections over several generations practising many vanishing crafts and trades.

BEDFORDSHIRE'S YESTERYEARS Vol. 4:
War Times and Civil Matters:
Brenda Fraser-Newstead.
Two World Wars, plus transport, law and order, etc.

THE CHANGING FACE OF LUTON: An Illustrated History:
Stephen Bunker, Robin Holgate and Marian Nichols.
Luton's development from earliest times to the present busy industrial town. Illustrated in colour and monochrome. The three authors from Luton Museum are all experts in local history, archaeology, crafts and social history.

THE MEN WHO WORE STRAW HELMETS:
Policing Luton, 1840–1974: Tom Madigan.
Meticulously chronicled history; dozens of rare photographs; author served in Luton Police for nearly fifty years.

BETWEEN THE HILLS:
The Story of Lilley, a Chiltern Village: Roy Pinnock.
A priceless piece of our heritage – the rural beauty remains but the customs and way of life described here have largely disappeared.

GLEANINGS REVISITED:
Nostalgic Thoughts of a Bedfordshire's Farmer's Boy:
E W O'Dell.
His own sketches and early photographs adorn this lively account of rural Bedfordshire in days gone by.

FARM OF MY CHILDHOOD, 1925–1947: Mary Roberts.
An almost vanished lifestyle on a remote farm near Flitwick.

THE VALE OF THE NIGHTINGALE:
The True Story of a Harpenden Family: Molly Andrews.
Victorian times to the present day in this lovely village.

THE TALL HITCHIN SERGEANT:
A Victorian Crime Novel based on fact:
Edgar Newman.
Mixes real police officers and authentic background with an exciting storyline.

THE TALL HITCHIN INSPECTOR'S CASEBOOK:
A Victorian Crime Novel based on fact:
Edgar Newman.
Worthies of the time encounter more archetypal villains.

LEAFING THROUGH LITERATURE: Writer's Lives
in Hertfordshire and Bedfordshire:
David Carroll.
Illustrated short biographies of many famous authors and their connections with these counties.

THE HILL OF THE MARTYR: An Architectural History
of St. Albans Abbey: Eileen Roberts.
Scholarly and readable chronological narrative history of Hertfordshire and Bedfordshire's famous cathedral. Fully illustrated with photographs and plans.

SPECIALLY FOR CHILDREN

VILLA BELOW THE KNOLLS:
A Story of Roman Britain:
Michael Dundrow.
An exciting adventure for young John in Totternhoe and Dunstable two thousand years ago.

ADVENTURE ON THE KNOLLS:
A Story of Iron Age Britain:
Michael Dundrow.
Excitement on Totternhoe Knolls as ten-year-old John finds himself back in those dangerous times, confronting Julius Caesar and his army.

THE RAVENS:
One Boy Against the Might of Rome:
James Dyer.
On the Barton Hills and in the south-east of England as the men of the great fort of Ravensburgh (near Hexton) confront the invaders.

Further titles are in preparation.
All the above are available via any bookshop, or from the publisher and bookseller

THE BOOK CASTLE
12 Church Street, Dunstable Bedfordshire, LU5 4RU
Tel: (01582) 605670

Autographs

Autographs

Autographs

Autographs

Autographs

Autographs

Autographs

Autographs

Autographs

Autographs

Autographs